POLYMER CLAY
SURFACE DESIGN RECIPES

QUARRY

POLYMER CLAY
SURFACE DESIGN RECIPES
100 Mixed-Media Techniques Plus Projects Ideas

GLOUCESTER MASSACHUSETTS

QUARRY BOOKS

Ellen Marshall

First published in the United States of America by
Quarry Books, a member of
Quayside Publishing Group
33 Commercial Street
Gloucester, Massachusetts 01930-5089
Telephone: (978) 282-9590
Fax: (978) 283-2742
www.rockpub.com

Chapter 1 is adapted from *Polymer Clay: Exploring New
Techniques and New Materials* (Rockport Publishers, 2002),
by Georgia Sargeant and Celie Fago.

Library of Congress Cataloging-in-Publication Data
Marshall, Ellen.
    Polymer clay surface design recipes : 100 mixed-media
techniques plus project ideas / Ellen Marshall.
        p.   cm.
    ISBN 1-59253-171-7 (pbk.)
    1. Polymer clay craft. I. Title.
TT297.M33 2005
731.4'2—dc22
                                        2005003453
                                        CIP

ISBN 1-59253-171-7

10 9 8 7 6 5 4 3 2

Design: Susan Raymond Art & Design

All photography by Allan Penn except pages 17 and 19
by Bobbie Bush/www.bobbiebush.com

Printed in Singapore

To Aine and Emaleigh who inspire me in all that I do.

To the Philadelphia Area Polymer Clay Guild: Thank you all for your support. It is great to be among you.

Contents

Introduction

ENJOY!

My passion for polymer clay started innocently enough. A little over a decade ago, I read about polymer clay in a sewing magazine and how it could be used to make buttons to embellish clothing. I never made those buttons. In fact, I didn't do very much with the sampler set I bought. I simply didn't know much about working with the material.

In time, I learned that there was a vast and varied repertoire of polymer clay techniques and manipulations to consider. There was caning, sculpting, imitative techniques, fiber art approaches, and certainly a smattering of surface techniques. In addition, I discovered the National Polymer Clay Guild and a community of artists who collectively promote polymer clay as an artistic medium. This led me to gather others to found the Philadelphia Area Polymer Clay Guild, and more recently, the Mixed Media Design Group. You might say that all of this has just been the result of unbridled enthusiasm.

This passion was further fueled, as I started teaching polymer clay classes. I modestly intended to teach fun and interesting projects, but I discovered that I could inspire others to try working with polymer clay or try new ways of doing so. More important, I found that others inspired me to continue to learn and experiment artistically. I am grateful to the people who have taken my classes for the powerful connections we have made.

So I come to writing this book, which is the result of my artistic journey thus far. It is intended for artists who work primarily with polymer clay—or not. It is clear today that whether we identify ourselves as being beaders, quilt artists, rubber stampers, sewers, or polymer artists, we have something to share with one another. More and more we are playing in each other's backyards, and the art that is emerging from this is astonishing.

I hope this book gives you ideas and helps you make artistic discoveries. Your passion for art may have started simply too. What a joy it is to revel in now!

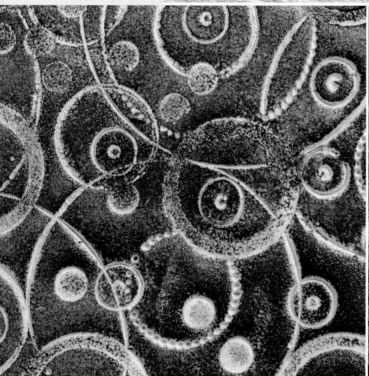

A Helpful Note to Readers

This book presents a wide array of techniques and inspirations for creating unique surface designs in polymer clay. We have made an attempt to tell you very specifically what materials we have used to get a particular effect, so that if desired, you can try to duplicate a result exactly. If a product has a certain property or characteristic that makes it especially suitable for a particular effect, we have made a point to tell you. In many cases, another brand may work just as well, but we still tell you exactly what we used, in case you want to match a particular color or design.

Please note: None of this specificity should discourage you from substituting similar products that are easier to find or that you may already have. You may discover that your results are exactly the same, or you may find completely unexpected results that make you just as happy. We have tried to design this book so that the information provided, based on the author's extensive experience and testing, is as detailed and as helpful as we can make it, but we also encourage you to conduct your own experimentation and to not feel limited by the suggested products in any way.

A majority of the materials used in this book are available internationally or can be easily ordered on the Internet. A resources section is included for your reference on page 123.

Chapter 1
Getting Started

A Guide to Using this Book

I hope you find this book inspiring and informative whether you are familiar with polymer clay or not . If you are already acquainted with surface design from the paper or textile arts, I hope you will see surface techniques in a new light. One goal of this book is to illustrate how anyone interested in surface design, regardless of their experience, can develop or expand their repertoire of surface treatments by using artist media in different ways and by combining surface and polymer clay techniques. Stamps can be used to apply images or texture. Paints and inks can be used in silk-screening, mono-printing, or masking. Acrylic media can be used to create faux suede, raku, or paste paper surfaces. The other goal of this book is to spark ideas for using surface design. There are a number of creative designs in the project and gallery sections of this book. From a simple card (page 84) to an elaborate necklace with beaded fringe (page 88), you'll find a variety of ways to use decorated clay in creating mixed-media pieces of art.

Polymer clay is our foundation material, so we begin this chapter with an overview of the material and methods for working with it. To create successful surface designs, it is important to become familiar with the properties of different media and how they interact with clay. Information about how particular materials, such as paints, inks, and acrylic media, work on clay is given in the technique and project instructions.

It is difficult to provide blanket rules about how artist materials work on clay. For example, acrylic paints and inks generally dry on raw or unbaked clay and bond permanently to clay when baked. But not all acrylic paints and inks dry completely on raw clay; some remain a little tacky. There is a variation in how products perform because manufacturers use different formulations. This is actually a welcome fact. It is precisely because of the differences in how materials work with clay that result in not only the surface techniques you'll find in this book, but also the techniques you may discover as you try various ideas. Note, too, that new products are being introduced to the market constantly, which offer the opportunity to create new techniques or apply current ones in different ways.

In my favorite section, Surface Technique Intensives (page 60), I invite you to use your surface-design knowledge and work with abandon. Mix materials! Mix techniques! Do the unthinkable—cut up that breathtaking decorated sheet you've just made! You'll appreciate how working in this way can fuel your creativity.

About Polymer Clay

Polymer clay is a brilliantly colored modern modeling material that bakes hard in a home oven. Its star feature is its compatibility with other art and craft materials, from acrylic paints to glues to glitter to metal leafing to rubber-stamping supplies. With polymer clay widely available in art and craft stores, sturdy and colorful three-dimensional art is within everyone's reach.

The basic ingredient of polymer clay is polyvinyl chloride (PVC), the same sturdy stuff that water pipes are made of. It also contains inert fillers to give it bulk (and sometimes texture), dyes and pigments to give it color, and a plasticizer—an oily chemical that allows the microscopic chains of PVC molecules to slide over each other at room temperature but lock onto each other when the clay is heated.

This clay, also known to its fans as "polyclay" and "PC," comes in many of the colors you find on the artist's paint rack—not only standard colors like red, white, and brown, but also flesh tones (developed for doll making) and translucents which are milky when raw but almost clear when baked properly (and in a thin enough layer, they're absolutely transparent). With many brands, you can mix the package colors and get attractive intermediate shades.

Manufacturers also make some wonderful specialty clays. There are pearlescent and metallic colors that incorporate tiny mica flakes to provide a shimmery luster. There are clays that remain flexible and rubbery and act like a pencil eraser when baked. There are glow-in-the-dark colors that shine at night. You can even make your own stone clays by mixing embossing powder from the rubber-stamp counter into translucent clay. Or you can mix in other grains or powders, from coffee grounds to aromatic herbs to iridescent pigments to children's tinted play sand.

With this book you'll learn many techniques for decorating the surface of opaque, translucent, and metallic clays. But feel free to experiment with other custom-color and specialty clays. The only rule in working with polymer clay is to create joyously!

Polymer Clay Basics

Which Clay Should You Use?

Polymer clay is colorful, adaptable, and compatible with many other art and craft materials. It's heat sensitive, which means it's stiff when cold and more malleable when warm. As you knead and condition it, especially by hand, it gets warmer, softer, and stickier, but it does firm up again when it cools.

The different brands on the market are similar enough to be blended successfully, but they do have different characteristics. When you become familiar with the various properties of each, it will be easy to choose the right clay for the job. Manufacturers do change clay formulas from time to time, and they're always releasing new products, so test clays yourself to discover your favorites.

❖ **Sculpey** is an inexpensive, soft, brittle, white clay that is popular with railroad and dollhouse modelers for making buildings and landscape figures that will not receive wear and tear. It takes paint well.

❖ **Premo Sculpey** is a fine, all-purpose clay that is strong and slightly flexible when properly baked. Many of the colors are the same as artist's paint colors, making paint-mixing savvy useful. It's a good caning clay. Some sculptors and doll makers find it too soft and sticky.

❖ **Sculpey III** bakes to an attractive matte finish, and its translucent clay becomes the clearest of all. It's often given to children because it's soft

out of the package. However, it can accidentally "toast," or turn brown, if the oven temperature is too high. Even when properly baked, it's relatively chalky and brittle and breaks easily if dropped.

❖ **Sculpey Super Flex** is a very soft, sticky clay when uncured that remains highly flexible even after it's baked. When making a mold from an existing object, ensure the clay won't stick to the object by first coating the clay with a release agent, such as cornstarch, baby powder, talcum powder, water, or glycerin.

❖ **Super Sculpey** is a very strong, hard clay designed for doll making. It's sold only in large packages.

❖ **Fimo Classic** is a firm clay, valued by cane makers for its ability to hold fine patterns and by sculptors for its ability to take sharp details and hold its shape.

❖ **Fimo Soft** is firm in the package, but it is pressure-sensitive, so it softens readily under a roller. The transparent colors are brilliant, like stained glass. The glitter colors are made from tinted transparent clay blended with fine, heat-tolerant glitter.

❖ **Cernit** is formulated for doll making. It's soft to handle, but it's the hardest of the polymer clays when cured. Most colors are slightly translucent, like porcelain.

❖ **Creall-Therm** is excellent for making miniatures because it can safely be rolled out into tiny threads without breaking, and it isn't overly sticky.

❖ **Kato Clay** is the newest clay on the market. This clay conditions easily and is strong and durable when cured. The clay is also good for caning, and it requires less sanding and buffing to achieve a polished finish.

Fimo, Kato, and Sculpey all make a translucent liquid clay. Kato liquid clay (also known as **Kato Sauce**) and **Translucent Liquid Sculpey** (TLS) are products used in this book primarily as a finish to seal powders or crayon on the surface of clay. Liquid translucent clay has a variety of decorative and utilitarian uses. Powders, alcohol, acrylic inks, and oil-based artist paint can be mixed into TLS and applied on clay as a paint or glaze. Mix oil-based paint in liquid clay for consistent results. You can get bubbling or crackle effects when baking liquid clay mixed with acrylic paint depending of the grade and chemistry of the paint. Liquid clay can also be used to fill in small crevices or to assure adhesion between baked and unbaked clay. See the section about sanding and buffing liquid clay to a glasslike shine (see page 26).

Polymer Clay Equipment and Supplies

Experiment and you'll soon discover which tools work best for you. Below are the essential items you'll need to begin, including some household items adaptable for use with polymer clay.

Safety Tip: Polymer clay is certified nontoxic, so it's safe for adults and supervised children to use. However, once you use a kitchen tool with polymer clay, don't use it for preparing food again, and don't place foods on polymer clay surfaces.

Basic Kit (shown on right)

❖ **Work surface (A)** You'll need a large, smooth, and solvent-proof work area as your base. It can be made of Lucite, tempered glass, marble, tile, Formica, (or similar kitchen counter material); a flexible polypropylene plastic cutting board, or even heavy paper or cardboard will work. Don't use a varnished tabletop; as raw clay will damage varnish and acrylic plastics such as those used for inexpensive picture frames. Bare wood isn't ideal either because clay will stick in the pores. If you use paper for your work area, you'll need a separate cutting surface made from Lucite, glass, or a self-healing craft cutting board.

❖ **Rolling tools (B)** An acrylic pipe or rod, a brayer, a heavyweight straight-sided drinking glass or jar, a thick wooden dowel, or a marble rolling pin will all work. To make large, even, thin sheets, a pasta machine is extremely helpful.

❖ **Cutting tools (C)** Sharp scissors with smooth blades, craft knives with pointed and rounded blades, and long, thin tissue blades specially made for polymer clay are all useful.

❖ **Needle tools (D)** These are available from ceramics suppliers and can also be found in the sculpting section of art supply stores. You can also make your own by placing a large darning needle in a polymer clay ball, baking it, then pulling out the needle, washing off any oil, and gluing it back in place with cyanoacrylate glue.

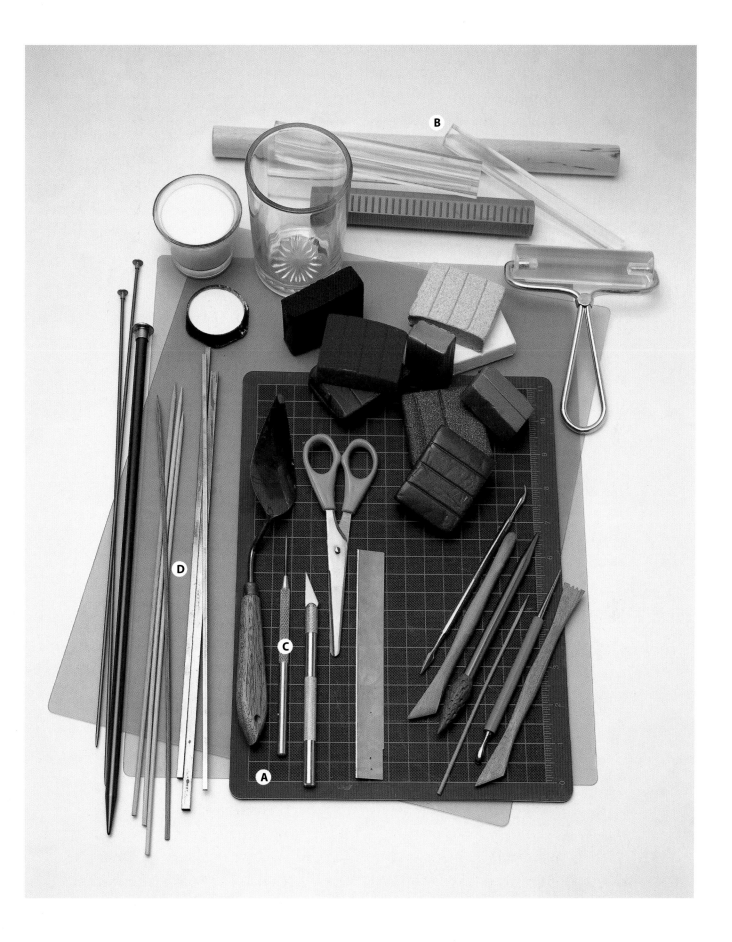

❖ **Oven** When you're first getting to know polymer clay, a home oven may be used, then wiped out and washed down carefully afterward. Once hooked, most cautious clay lovers obtain a small portable toaster oven or convection oven and use it only for art.

❖ **Oven thermometer** To properly cure polymer clay, you'll need a thermometer to check and calibrate your oven's temperature.

❖ **Rubbing alcohol** Tools and surfaces can be cleaned easily with rubbing alcohol.

❖ **Finishing materials** Sanding with wet/dry sandpaper followed by buffing with a cotton wheel gives polymer clay a polished, glasslike finish. You'll need sandpaper grits ranging from 320 to 600, which you can buy from home-improvement stores. For an even shinier finish, extrafine grades from 800 to 2,000 are available at auto-supply stores.

❖ **Latex or plastic gloves** Polymer clay is certified nontoxic, but like all art materials, it should be used with care. Some people find that it irritates their skin, so protect your hands with latex or plastic gloves or an artist's or mechanic's cream.

Safety Tip: Tissue blades are extremely sharp, and the dull and cutting edges look similar. Paint the dull side with nail polish, or bake a strip of polymer clay onto it, remove the clay, then glue this new "handle" into place on the tissue blade.

Intermediate Kit

Shown on page 19 are some of the things that can also be used with polymer clay. Many of the items pictured are called for in the techniques and projects that follow. Once you've assembled a basic kit, start experimenting with other materials to assemble a more sophisticated, personalized kit.

Working With Polymer Clay

Conditioning

Polymer clay can be used right out of the package, but conditioning the clay makes it more pliable. (Some artists say that conditioning also makes it stronger.) During conditioning, the plasticizer is distributed more evenly, bubbles are driven out, and the clay warms up and softens. When it cools, it will firm up again, but the other improvements will remain.

To condition clay by hand, it's best to start with the clay at body temperature. To get it there, you can put the packages in your clothing for a while, place them in a gentle warming device such as a baby-bottle warmer or a barely warm heating pad, or seal them in a resealable plastic bag and submerge the bag in lukewarm water.

Remove the wrapper and lay about 1 oz (28 gm) of clay (half a block) on your work surface. Roll over it heavily with a strong roller: an acrylic rod or pipe, a brayer, a thick wooden dowel, or a rolling pin. (An acrylic rod is preferable because clay will not stick to it with repeated use.) Fold it, squash it flat, and roll again. When it's a bit softer, form it into a log, and roll it out into a snake. Fold it over, twist it, and ball it up. Repeat until the clay has the texture and elasticity you want—approximately fifteen to twenty times.

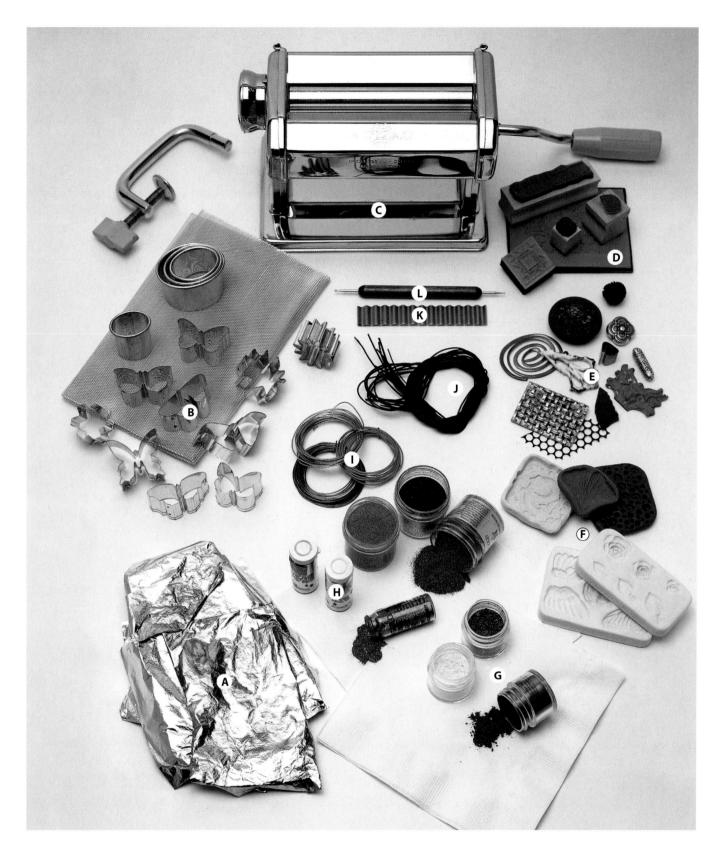

A metallic leaf

B cookie and hors d'ouevres cutters

C pasta machine (durable Italian model)

D deep-cut rubber stamps

E texturing tools, such as beads, charms, and found objects

F molds, handmade and commercial

G powders and pigments, such as metallic, mica, and embossing powders

H inclusions, such as ultrafine glitters and tiny beads

I plastic-coated craft wire

J rubber and leather cording

K wavy blade

L ball-end stylus

To condition clay with a pasta machine, lay half a block of clay on your work surface and flatten it to make it thin enough to feed into the pasta machine's rollers. Crank it through. Fold the resulting sheet in half and feed it through again, fold side first. Repeat about twenty times.

It takes the same amount and kind of work to mix colors uniformly as is does to condition clay. If you want to mix colors, begin when you start conditioning.

Leaching

Clay that is fresh from the factory may be too soft and sticky to work with. To harden it a bit, roll it into sheets (using the middle setting on a pasta machine). Place the sheets on clean office paper, then sandwich them between absorbent newspapers, and weigh them down with books for at least 24 hours. Some of the oily plasticizer will leach into the papers. In some cases, you may have to do this more than once before the clay is firm enough.

Softening

All clay becomes firmer over time, as polymerization slowly advances. Some clays are inherently stiffer than others. Two proprietary softeners—Sculpey Diluent or Clay Softener and Fimo Mix Quick—can be used to soften clay that is too hard. Artists have also used vegetable oil or mineral oil. The translucent liquid clays can also be used for this purpose. You can mix any brand of liquid clay with any brand of solid clay, but you may develop a preference for a particular combination.

First, chop up the hard clay, place it in a resealable plastic bag, add a few drops of softener, and leave it to soak overnight. The next day, compress the bag to adhere the clay scraps together. Take them out and place them on a sheet of fresh clay, fold the sheet around the scraps, and condition the whole "sandwich."

Storing Opened Packages

Don't leave raw clay on a painted or varnished surface, because the plasticizer will mar the surface. Instead, store the clay in the original package, a resealable plastic bag, or a polyethylene shoebox, which protects the clay from dust.

Baking

Each manufacturer provides specifications for baking, or curing, their brand of polymer clay properly so that it hardens and fuses throughout without burning. These specifications are printed on the packages, and they vary from brand to brand. If the directions are missing, a good rule of thumb is to bake your clay project for thirty minutes per 1/4" (6 mm) of thickness at 265°F to 275°F (129°C to 135°C). Some of the translucent clays may brown at this temperature, so first bake a test tile the same thickness as your project.

Most ovens cycle, first heating above the designated temperature, then turning off the heat and cooling down, then heating again, so most oven thermometers are inaccurate. To control the temperature, preheat the oven and use a separate oven thermometer to calibrate it: Adjust the dial on the oven until the oven thermometer reads 265°F (129°C), and don't worry about what the dial says.

If your oven has an overhead heating element, you may want to protect your project from scorching with an aluminum foil tent. The clay shouldn't go above 300°F (149°C), because it will begin to scorch and emit unpleasant fumes.

During baking, the clay goes through a soft stage when it can sag or slump under gravity and conform to the surface supporting it. To prevent this, thin strands or sheets should be supported with a curl of paper, and to avoid getting glassy spots where the clay piece touched a polished glass or metal baking surface, it's a good idea to lay the clay on a piece of plain paper or cardboard for baking.

Beads can be set on pleated paper or cardstock, which will yield while supporting them; or they can be held up on a bamboo skewer, a stiff wire, or 00 aluminum knitting needles. Large rounded objects can be supported during baking by a nest of quilt stuffing, which won't melt or stick to the clay.

Ceramic tiles make an excellent, inexpensive, portable baking surface, and they're available in both glossy and matte finishes. Many clayers bake on metal or tempered glass pans or sheets of cardboard. Don't bake on Teflon, which can fuse with polymer clay.

After baking, most projects should be allowed to cool slowly to room temperature. But translucent clay benefits from being dropped into ice water while still hot; if you do this, the final project will appear more translucent.

Safety Tip: Bake polymer clay with the best ventilation you can manage. Turn on a fan and open the windows.

Cleaning Up

Your work surface and pasta machine should be kept clean to avoid having one color of clay contaminate the next one. Many clayers wipe down their machines with baby wipes or rubbing alcohol on a paper towel.

The warmer your hands, the more likely they are to acquire a sticky film of clay as you work. Massaging in a bit of hand lotion and wiping it off with a paper towel, then washing with cool water and dish detergent that cuts grease should do the trick.

Choosing Glue

PVA-Based White Craft Glues

Use this basic glue to help raw clay bond to baked clay or stick to paper. PVA stands for polyvinyl acetate, a close chemical cousin to the PVC (polyvinyl chloride) that is the basis of polymer clay. Coat the cured surface with the glue and allow it to dry, then affix the raw clay.

Cyanoacrylate Glue

This glue, commonly called SuperGlue or Krazy Glue, can be used to bond baked clay to metal, glass, or other pieces of baked clay. The cyanoacrylate glue bond fails at high temperatures, however, there is now an exception to this: Poly Bonder by Lisa Pavelka, Heart in Hand Studio, is effective up to 300°F (149°C).

E6000 Silicon Glue

This heavy-duty glue is extremely effective, but it contains harsh solvents. Use it outdoors.

Two-Part Epoxy Glues

These are the best glues for bonding baked clay to metal, such as jewelry findings.

Basic Techniques

Making Sheets

All the surface techniques in this book require that you make polymer clay sheets. The easiest way to control this is to pinch and pull your conditioned clay into a rough rectangle about the thickness of a dinner plate, then roll it through a pasta machine, which is designed to roll out even, consistent layers of dough. Pasta machines take so much of the labor out of clay work that they're well worth the investment— and they can often be found at secondhand stores and yard sales.

But even if you don't have a pasta machine, you can still make thin, even sheets by using bakers' techniques and treating your clay like piecrust dough. With your hands, roll a lump of conditioned clay into a fat cylinder, dust it with cornstarch or talc, and flatten it with a thick roller. You can pull on the edges with your hands to help the process.

To roll the clay out to an even thickness, tape down two long rods, skewers, or chopsticks beside the clay in a parallel orientation. (Many hobby shops sell foot-long sections of squared-off brass and aluminum tubing in different diameters that would be ideal for this.) Place the roller on top of the rod and roll out the clay that is positioned between them. You can get clay sheets that vary in thickness by varying the thickness of the rods. Then roll your clay out even with the rods.

Settings for Rolling Sheets

This chart, devised by Dottie McMillan, lists the corresponding thickness for each pasta machine setting. (Some machines have more than seven settings.) It is a useful guide when you need to prepare relatively thick or thin sheets.

Setting	Inches	Millimeters
1	$\frac{1}{8}$ "	3.2 mm
2	$\frac{7}{64}$ "	2.8 mm
3	$\frac{3}{32}$ "	2.4 mm
4	$\frac{5}{64}$ "	2.0 mm
5	$\frac{1}{16}$ "	1.6 mm
6	$\frac{1}{32}$ "	0.8 mm
7	$\frac{1}{40}$ "	0.6 mm

Millefiori (Canework)

One of the most popular polymer clay techniques comes from the clay's ability to stretch evenly and smoothly. It shares this quality, technically known as "thixotropicity," with hot glass and hard candy. This stretchiness makes it possible to layer several colors together in a pattern, consolidate the layers into a multicolored loaf, then stretch out the loaf without changing the proportions of the colors.

Long pieces of different-colored polymer clay can be assembled into many-colored "canes" that keep the same pattern throughout the length, even after you compress the sides and stretch the cane out long and narrow. This is called "reducing" the cane—really you're reducing the diameter but increasing the length. The great thing is that with clay, you can do it all at room temperature! And once you have made a cane, you can make many thin slices with the same pattern, just as slicing a jellyroll dessert yields the same spiral pattern in every slice. In fact, one of the most common canes is called a "jellyroll" cane.

Cane patterns can be as simple as stripes, checks, bull's-eyes, and swirls. And because you can stack and pack simple canes together, they can also add up to complex canes of flowers, faces, and even landscapes. A combination of simple and complex canes are displayed in Clay as Surface Media, page 54.

Color Mixing, Marbling, and Blends

You can mix two or more colors during the conditioning process simply by flattening each color and stacking the layers at the start; by the time you have finished conditioning, the colors will be mixed.

One of the simplest decorative techniques is to marble clay. Start by making small snakes of different colors of conditioned clay. Bundle them, pack them, and twist them together. Roll the bundle on your work surface to lengthen it, then fold it and twist again. Stop when you like the marbled effect; if you go too far, the clay will start to look blended rather than marbled.

For a simple blend—often called "Skinner blend" in reference to the technique's developer, Judith

Skinner—start by rolling out two colors of clay sheets about the same size. (The clay doesn't have to be conditioned in advance, because it will be conditioned by the blending process.) Trim them into rectangles. Slice one sheet diagonally, and stack the two triangles; repeat with the other sheet. Butt the two double triangles together so they make a rectangle, one color on each side; overlap the edge a bit, and press them so they stick together. Feed the double-thick rectangle through the rollers of a pasta machine. This will stretch out the rectangle twice as long but a single thickness. Fold it in half again at the "waist," and roll it through again, fold side first. Repeat about fifteen times, always folding at the waist and sending it through fold side first. By the time you have finished, you'll have a smooth color blend with one color down one vertical edge and the other color down the other vertical edge; the upper and lower edges will show the blend. If you stop early—after about ten times—you'll have an incomplete blend with a cross-section that looks streaky, like ikat cloth.

For a complex blend, start by rolling out a clay sheet at least 6" (15 cm) long in each color you want to use. From each sheet, cut out two long triangles about 2" (5 cm) wide at the base. Assemble them together, head to foot, into a rectangle the width of your pasta machine; overlap the edges of the pieces, and pinch them together. Send the whole piece through the pasta machine. Fold the long rectangle at the "waist," and send it through the pasta machine, fold side first. Repeat as above. You'll have a blended sheet with one color down one side, another down the other side; the top and bottom edges will show the blend. The ikat technique and complex color blending are shown in the final surface treatment on page 74.

Metallic Effects

Some of the Premo Sculpey clays contain so much mica that they look like mother-of-pearl or metal. Mica is formed of flat plates, and remarkably, when you run the metallic or pearl clays through the pasta machine, the pressure seems to make the plates line up and face the surface of the sheet. Because the little plates reflect light, the surface looks brighter and brighter the more you send it through the pasta machine. Conversely, the edges of the sheet look darker because you're looking between the little plates.

Acrylic floor finish and metallic powders are used to create a crackled effect on the handle of this ice cream scoop.

Artist: Mona Kissel

Artists discovered this effect and figured out many ways to use it. Most rely on making sheets of brightened clay, cutting them into uniform pieces, stacking them, and then manipulating the stack in various ways to take advantage of the contrast between the brightened surface and the darkened edges.

Mokumé Gané

An ancient Japanese metalworking technique inspired the artists who developed these methods. The original involved soldering and compressing layers of several colored metals into one fused piece, punching into them from both sides to make bumps and hollows, then sanding off the bumps to reveal the layers beneath.

In clay, of course, it's easy to get different layers to stick together, and clay artists have a rainbow of colors, translucents, pearly clays, paints, inclusions, and metal leaf to work with. Many artists have developed special variations on this theme. Layer work shows how different artists can take a basic idea, play with it, and come up with utterly different results.

The core mokumé gané technique is to stack different colored sheets of unbaked clay, rumple them like a bed after a restless night or punch into them, then take thin slices from the top. Because the layers are no longer flat, each cut will slice through several layers, revealing striations the way a road cut reveals underlying layers of earth and stone or a wood carver reveals the grain of a block of wood. Often these irregular slices are flipped over, laid on another sheet of clay, and rolled down to create a variegated sheet. This can be used as is or made into a veneer to cover an object. Depending on which clays are originally selected and whether other materials such as glitter or metal leaf are included, the effects can be very different.

Using Armatures, Inside and Out

Polymer clay is malleable until cured, and it becomes even softer for a short time during baking. Small objects usually aren't heavy enough to go out of shape during baking, but heat and gravity will make sheets and large items sag unless they're supported.

Heavy paper and cardboard can be used externally—for example, a stiff paper cone can be wrapped in a floppy sheet of clay, which will be sturdy once it has been baked. Heat-resistant materials can be used internally as armatures. Glass and most metals are suitable. Crushed aluminum foil makes a good core for sculptures and beads. Metal screening can be used to reinforce thin sheets.

With successive bakings, clay itself can become a kind of armature. After the foundation layer is baked, it becomes stiff and easy to handle; later layers can be added and baked, permitting the construction of elaborate objects. A tiny dab of translucent liquid clay on points that may be stressed later will help ensure a solid bond.

Covering Forms

When a sheet of clay is wrapped or draped over a glass, metal, wood, or cardboard form and then baked, the clay takes on that shape. You can use found objects such as bottles, bowls, boxes, lighting fixtures, switch plates, or tins as forms, or you can build your own with tape and cardboard. Keep in mind that manipulating decorated sheets of clay over a form can distort or destroy the surface treatment. Minimize this by applying decorated clay to simple forms or apply decorated clay as individual tiles. You may bake between each tile's application to ensure that the decoration is preserved.

If you don't want the clay and the form to stick together after baking, use a release agent between them. Pull the clay and form apart while they're still hot from baking; clay expands very little when hot, but that little can be helpful in separating tightly fitted pieces. If you're willing to leave the form in place, simple enclosure will hold them together. If you don't want to leave it in, you can cut the clay (preferably an angled cut), pull out the form, and then use glue or translucent liquid clay to reunite the cuts. Don't use varnished or painted metal as a form without a lot of release agent; the clay will stick to the varnish. Conversely, painted tins can easily be permanently covered with clay because it sticks to the paint.

Finishing Touches

Carving, Drilling, and Filing

Once fully baked, polymer clay can be easily carved, incised, filed, sawed, or drilled. Underbaked clay is usually too brittle to withstand this treatment. Experiment with woodcarving tools, sculpting tools, and any other kind of implement you can find at art- and craft-supply stores. Once carved, try rubbing paint into the grooves to accentuate them.

To drill a thin or small piece of polymer clay, mark the area first, and use a needle tool to gently dent the area. Then, simply hand-twist a drill bit into the dent to enlarge it. For thicker or larger pieces of clay, use a small hobby drill.

Artist's Tip: Incised or cut areas will likely appear white, but this residue can be removed by rebaking the piece. Alternately, the incised areas could be back-filled with clay or tube acrylic paint. You should rebake after back-filling with either clay or paint.

Polishing

Polishing translucent clay is especially effective, because the transparency is greatly enhanced. When transparent liquid clay is applied over a surface treatment, the resulting baked surface may be sanded and buffed to a polished finish. But consider this step carefully, as the coating of liquid clay is thin and you don't want to sand away any of your decorative finish. You can apply more liquid clay to the piece and bake it again.

If you choose to sand and buff your piece, here are the general directions for doing so. When working with wet/dry sandpaper, always use it in water (a full bowl will do it) to keep the clay cool and the dust in the water, so you don't inhale it. If you want to remove a lot of clay, start at 180 grit (fairly coarse), then progress to 320, 400, and 600 grit; if you want a real shine, get superfine paper (800 grit and higher) at an auto-supply shop. Finally, buff it on your jeans or other cotton cloth until glossy. Aficionados may want to use

a bench grinder with an unstitched cotton wheel or even a variable speed buffer made for jewelers. Buffing attachments are available for hobby drills.

Artist's Tip: Keep the clay object moving at all times. If you let it linger too long in one spot on the buffing wheel, the friction could damage the clay.

Artist: Gwen Gibson

The decorated clay on this pin (left) and wearable box pendant (above) was created with handmade silk screens and acrylic paint.

Chapter 2
Surface Techniques and Applications

If you're one to dive into new projects, then you've come to the right place. This chapter will guide you through familiar surface techniques that are created with some innovative twists, such as using a kitchen scrubbing sponge to stipple layers of oil pastel (below left) or monoprinting with facial tissue (below right).

 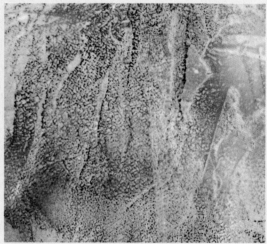

Stamping, a popular technique in general, is especially versatile when combined with polymer clay because not only color, but also texture come into play. Monoprinting, brayering, and masking are among the techniques for achieving different looks with paint or ink applications. Spraying, splattering, and sponging takes paint or ink in still another direction. Techniques involving powders, pastel crayons, and pens are also featured in conjunction with paint and ink methods as well as independently.

Note: White clay is the base for all tile swatches except where indicated. All clay is conditioned and rolled out to a medium thickness.

Surface techniques involving acrylic media can yield dramatic results. The techniques presented here introduce you to several acrylic products and faux surfaces that can be created with them. Imagine making faux suede or paste-paper ornaments! Clay as Surface Media (page 54) demonstrates that surface design on clay isn't only about applying *other* substances on clay.

The collection of Surface Technique Intensives (pages 60-81) gives you an opportunity to design surfaces using a combination of techniques. You can create either complex or subtle designs working this way. The choice is yours.

Whether you try the techniques in succession or work with them randomly, you'll gain a greater appreciation for the art of surface design.

 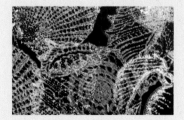 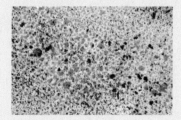

Basic Surface Recipes

Stamping to Add Images and Designs

Combining and applying stamps with various media allows for a wide array of effects.

Stamp credit: Stampendous

Materials

- beige or ecru clay
- opaque bronze metallic acrylic paint (shown: Lumiere)
- opaque copper metallic acrylic paint (shown: Lumiere)
- black acrylic gesso (shown: Golden)
- aluminum foil
- rubber stamp
- piece of a foam pad or a fine-textured cosmetic sponge

1. To prepare the background, use a piece of crumpled aluminum foil to stipple on a layer of bronze metallic paint. Let the paint dry. Repeat this step to apply another layer of copper metallic paint, and let it dry again.

2. Create a foam ink pad by applying black acrylic gesso to a section of foam pad.

3. Press the rubber stamp against the custom-made ink pad.

4. Stamp your design onto the stippled background of the polymer clay. Be sure to clean the stamp immediately.

Note: A fine-textured sponge is used predominately throughout this book except where indicated. You can use a sponge with different texture, but your results may vary.

Variations

1 Apply acrylic craft paint to plastic grids (found in the embroidery section of craft stores), course-weave embroidery-type cloth, and the prongs of a furniture coaster to create this collage of abstract images.

2 For extra contrast, use opaque metallic acrylic paints, such as any of the Stewart Gill lines or Jacquard's Lumiere, to stamp onto a background of black clay.

Stamp credit: Judikins

3 Smooth a light layer of mica powder onto the clay. Sponge an acrylic media, such as acrylic gel media or silk-screen media, onto a rubber stamp. After stamping, spray water on the stamp to keep the acrylic media from drying until the stamp can be cleaned. Smooth mica over the clay again to reveal the invisible images. Sponge Kato liquid translucent clay over the clay to seal the mica powder.

Stamp credit: Judikins

Basic Surface Recipes

Shadow and Bold Image Stamps

A dramatic overall image can be created with shadow and bold image stamps.

Stamp credits: Hero Arts; Hot Potatoes

Materials

- pigment ink palette set (shown: Clearsnap's ColorBox Fluid Chalk ink pad because of its ability to dry on polymer clay; Tsukineko's Brilliance is another pigment ink that similarly dries on clay)
- assortment of shadow and bold image stamps
- scrap of plain paper or paper towel

1. Lightly ink the shadow stamps (the squares) and a bold image stamp (the leaf) with colors from pigment ink palette set.

2. Stamp onto the clay, then gently blot the image with paper or a paper towel to remove excess ink and hasten the ink's drying. If you blot with a textured paper towel, a bit of the towel's texture will transfer.

Tip: The stamp may not adhere evenly on the clay and, as a result, the image may come out splotchy. You may like the look. If not, simply touch your finger to the ink pad and dab on more ink to fill in the splotches as desired.

Variations

1 Ink a bold image stamp with various colors of metallic acrylic paint, then stamp on the clay and smooth on mica powder. Create the border pattern by sponging on metallic paint. Use liquid translucent clay to seal the powder.

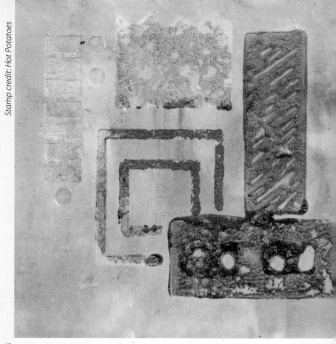

Stamp credit: Hot Potatoes

2 Here, preserve the detail of an intricate stamp by using Clearsnap's ColorBox Fluid Chalk ink pad.

Stamp credit: Hero Arts

3 Stamp this tile using acrylic ink (shown Dr. Ph. Martin's iridescent ink). Inks of this type cover the stamp and adhere to the clay differently than pigment inks or acrylic paints. As a result, this medium leaves lacelike images.

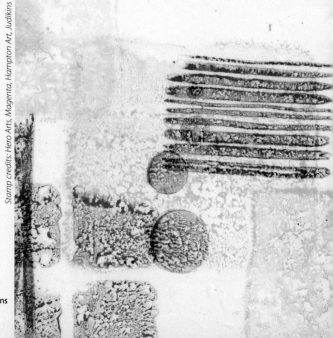

Stamp credits: Hero Arts, Magenta, Hampton Art, Judikins

Basic Surface Recipes

Stamps and Texture Tools

Stamps and texture tools provide dimensional interest to clay surfaces.

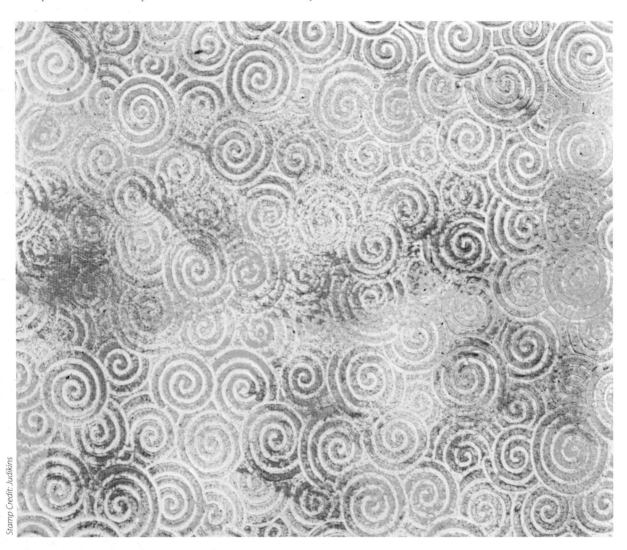

Stamp Credit: Judikins

Materials

- assortment of metallic and nonmetallic acrylic paints (shown: Jacquard's Textile Color)
- background or overall-pattern rubber stamp
- Armorall or spray bottle with water
- piece of a foam pad or a cosmetic sponge

1. Spritz the stamp with Armorall (car protectant finish) or water. This keeps the clay from sticking to the stamp.

2. Press the stamp into the clay to make an even impression.

3. Use the foam pad to lightly dab on one color of paint over the clay. Let the paint dry.

4. Apply additional layers of paint in a similar manner letting the paint dry after each layer.

Variations

1 Impress a texture sheet (shown: Shade-Tex) into brown clay to create a design. Sponge beige acrylic craft paint over the clay. Apply green, violet, and magenta metallic acrylic paint with a paintbrush and apply the magenta paint with small round sponge daubers.

Stamp Credit: Embossing Arts

2 Impress a daisy-patterned rubber stamp into a custom color of green clay. Sponge assorted acrylic paints onto the textured clay.

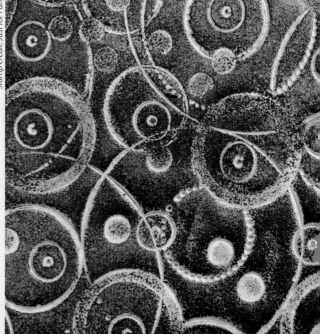

Stamp credit: Just for Fun

3 Sponge one color of acrylic paint over clay texturized with a rubber stamp.

Basic Surface Recipes

Monoprinting

Monoprinting emphasizes the interplay among paint or ink colors. Apply a minimum of colors to avoid creating a muddy mixture of paint or ink.

Materials

- metallic acrylic paint (shown: Stewart Gill's Pearlise and Byzantia)
- plastic sheet protector (found in craft and office supply stores)

1. Cut open a plastic sheet protector so it opens like a book.

2. Place a few dollops of metallic acrylic paint between the plastic pages. If you are using multiple colors, space each color widely because as the paints spread, some colors can be obscured.

3. Close the sheet protector and smooth your fingers over the plastic to spread the paint between the sheets.

4. Open the sheet protector and lay a sheet of clay over one or both sides of the protector.

5. Press your fingers over the clay to ensure the paint is picked up by the clay.

Variations

1 Spread dots of tube acrylic paint between the pages of a sheet protector. Lay the clay over the paint to apply.

> **Tip:** Spray a light mist of water over any acrylic paint or ink that starts drying on the sheet protector as you are working.

2 Place facial tissue between the pages of a sheet protector, then dot liquid acrylic paint or ink onto the tissue. (This is done so that if the liquid acrylic beads up on plastic, it would be absorbed by the tissue paper instead.) Lightly spray water over the tissue to help spread the liquid acrylic. Note how the folds in the tissue transfer as impressions in the color.

Stamp credit: Judikins

3 Dot Magic Color liquid acrylic directly onto the pages of a sheet protector. Fold the sheet protector and spread the liquid acrylic inside it. (This liquid acrylic does not bead up on the plastic.) Sprinkle a metallic powder (shown: Angelwing's Polished Pigments) over the spread of liquid acrylic, then layer the clay over the combination of media. The powder that adheres to the liquid acrylic will also adhere to the polymer clay.

Basic Surface Recipes

Masking

Masking on clay can be done with a variety of materials: paper, plastic film, metal wire, and low-tack or Post-it tape. If the masking material is impressed in the clay, you can create the look of dry embossing similar to paper with impressed images.

Materials

- assortment of acrylic craft paint (shown: Anita's)
- stencil plastic, acetate, or overhead projector sheet (shown: E-Z Cut plastic stencil)
- piece of a foam pad or cosmetic sponge
- jewelry tweezer
- scissors, regular or decorative cutting edge

1. Cut a piece of plastic into small sections. Place the plastic sections over the clay, leaving space between each section.

2. Sponge one of the colors all over the clay. You do not need to cover the clay entirely.

3. Let the paint layer dry.

4. Carefully pick up and reposition the plastic sections. Sponge another paint color over the clay. Let it dry.

5. Reposition the plastic sections and sponge on another layer of paint. Let it dry.

Variations

1 Make a mask of any shape out of artist vellum paper cut with decorative-edge scissors and apply D'uva ChromaCoal Sticks with the back of a section of foam. D'uva pastels can be slightly sticky on raw clay, but they fix permanently after the clay is baked.

2 Apply acrylic gloss gel media on black clay and let it dry. Place artist vellum paper masks cut with scissors and a spiral punch on the clay, and smooth the masks over the clay to secure them. Apply mica or pigment powders (shown: Angelwings' Polished Pigments, which are a combination of mica and pigment powders). Remove the stencils and bake the tile. Apply liquid clay to seal the powders and bake the tile again.

3 Layer Post-it tape onto the clay. Apply Crayola Portfolio water-soluble oil pastels with the abrasive side of a kitchen scrubbing sponge. Apply translucent liquid clay and bake.

Tip: Avoid leaving small clumps of the oil pastels on the clay. These might not get sealed under the liquid clay and will rub off.

Basic Surface Recipes

Brayering

Ink or paint can be applied with brayers to a smooth or textured finish.

Materials

- assortment of liquid acrylic paints (shown: Golden)
- rubber brayer

1. Place a few drops of the acrylic paints on the clay. Be careful not to use too many colors. They may become muddy when mixed.

2. Roll the brayer over part of the tile. Lift the brayer and roll it over another section of the tile.

3. Repeat this process to create a look you like.

Variations

1 Smooth a metallic powder onto clay. Roll a textured brayer in acrylic paint, then roll the brayer over the tile.

2 Apply Dye Na Flow fabric inks to a foam pad. Roll a rubber brayer over the pad, then roll it once over clay. Turn the clay 90 degrees, and roll the brayer once again.

3 Press a rubber stamp into clay. Roll a rubber brayer over a foam pad inked with Dye Na Flow fabric ink. Roll the brayer over the stamped clay several times to smooth the ink onto the clay. If you are using a rainbow of colors, be sure to keep the brayer aligned with the color stripes.

Stamp credit: Stamps Happen, Inc.

Basic Surface Recipes

Paste Paper

There are several acrylic gels and liquids available to try on polymer clay. Use acrylic media to create designs reminiscent of classic paste papers.

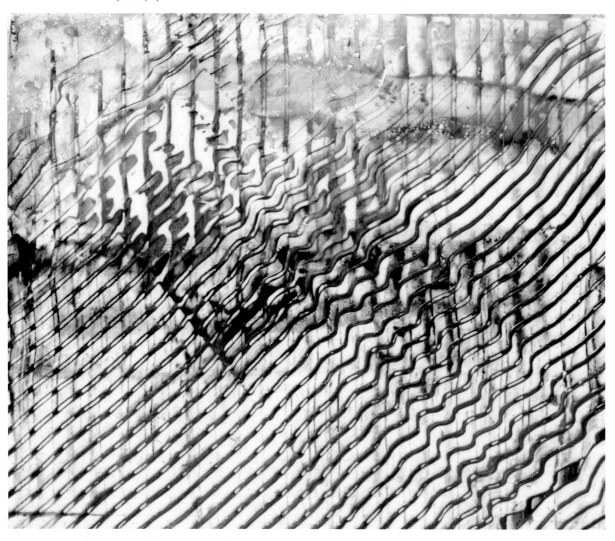

Materials

- assortment of liquid acrylic paints
- metal wood-graining combs
- small artist palette

1. Place lines of paint across the clay. The paint lines can touch or not.

2. Run a medium-tooth comb across the painted clay to spread the paint and to create classic paste-paper design.

3. Turn the clay diagonally and run a thin-tooth comb across it.

Variations

1 Mix drops of silk dye into a fluid acrylic medium. The amount varies according to how much mixture you need and how much color you want (shown: Colorhue dyes and Golden silk-screen medium). Smooth the mixture over clay. Comb a decorative pattern through the layer with a Coit multiline calligraphy pen.

2 Layer a mixture of liquid acrylic paint and acrylic gel medium over clay. Comb a decorative pattern through the layer with a wood-graining comb.

3 Smooth various colors of D'uva ChromaCoal pastel on clay. Layer on a mixture of liquid acrylic paint and acrylic gel medium, and comb through with two sizes of wood-graining combs.

Basic Surface Recipes

Acrylic Media

In "Paste Paper" acrylic gel effectively substitutes for the starch paste traditionally used to comb on paper. Here, two other acrylic compounds are used to affect the distribution of color.

Materials

- Golden Micaceous Iron Oxide acrylic medium (Linda Twohill coined the term "raku sauce" for this product.)
- oil pastels (used here: Crayola Portfolio)
- metallic powders
- palette knife or dinner knife
- small brush

1. Smooth the medium onto the clay with a knife and let it dry.

2. Brush metallic powders over the layer.

3. Rub oil pastels selectively over the surface. Smooth and blend the oil pastels as you apply them to complete the raku look.

Variations

1   Apply acrylic modeling paste on clay and let it dry. (shown: US ArtQuest 101 Light Artist's Medium. You could also use Golden modeling paste.) Sponge on various colors of acrylic craft paint.

2   For a different look, apply an opaque acrylic medium, such as US ArtQuest 101 Light Artist's Medium, leaving less texture, then let it dry. Paint al lover with one color of craft paint and apply additional colors sparingly.

3   Apply US ArtQuest 101 Heavy Artist's Medium (or Golden white gesso) on clay and let it dry. Dab on alcohol-based inks with cotton swabs or cosmetic applicators. Alcohol-based inks are fast-drying, yield dramatic blending effects, and have vibrant color (we used Ranger Crafts' Adirondack alcohol inks). Spritz on Adirondack alcohol blender solution, and while the surface is wet, sprinkle on metallic powders or dab with a metallic marker, such as Krylon, Sharpie, or Posh Impression markers.

Basic Surface Recipes

Silk-screening

Silk-screening is another way to transfer images—especially fine-lined or intricate ones—onto clay. Silk-screening results in a brocadelike finish on clay.

Materials

- fabric dye (shown: Colorhue)

- carrier medium (shown: Golden silk-screen medium, but a heavy hair gel containing alcohol can also be used)

- silk-screen stencil (used here: a stencil from the African series from Gwen Gibson)

- squeegee tool (used here: a wide Colour Shaper, but an old credit card or small rubber spatula can also be used)

- palette knife or a dinner knife

- foam plate or tray

- small spoon

- pan of cool water

1. Use a spoon to mix a few drops of the dye with a small amount of medium on a foam plate. Apply this mixture to the clay with a palette knife. Let it dry. Make a second color mixture.

2. Lay the stencil, shiny side down, onto the clay. Squeegee a small amount of the color mixture over the stencil. Lift the stencil and place it in the pan until you are ready to clean it.

Variations

1 Stencil metallic paint onto black clay (shown: Stewart Gill's Byzantia, which doesn't dry fully on the clay, but dries sufficiently for this application). When the first layer is dry, place a second stencil on the decorated clay. Spread tube acrylic paint across the second stencil. The opaque tube paint contrasts nicely with the more transparent metallic paint.

2 Spoon out small amounts of silk-screen medium on the plate. (Make a dollop for each color you are using; we used four colors.) Mix drops of the dye into the silk-screen medium, making individual color mixtures. Lay the stencil, shiny side down, onto the clay. Pick up a bit of one color mixture with a spoon and place bits of it on the stencil. Repeat with the remaining colors. Run the squeegee along the stencil, smoothing all the colors along the way. If there were sections of the clay left without color, clean off the squeegee and pick up color from the plate to correct this. This will keep your colors from getting muddy.

3 Sponge alcohol-based inks onto the clay with a cosmetic sponge. Lay the stencil over the clay, and squeegee tube acrylic paint across the stencil.

Basic Surface Recipes

Alcohol Inks

Alcohol inks blend like watercolors on polymer clay.

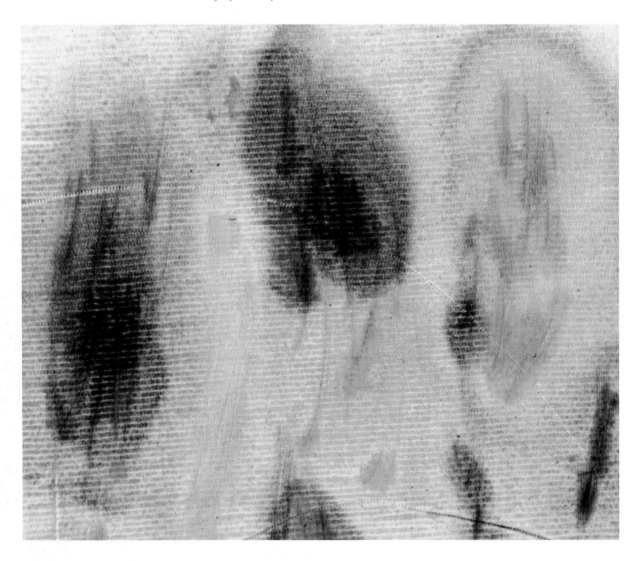

Materials

- alcohol-based inks, such as Ranger Crafts' Adirondack alcohol inks and Jacquard Piñata Colors
- swatch of fabric with a texture
- wax paper
- spray bottle containing rubbing alcohol
- brayer

1. Place the fabric on wax paper and spritz it lightly with alcohol.

2. Drop various colors of ink onto the fabric, allowing the colors to bleed into one another.

3. Pick up the fabric and wax paper together and place the fabric side on clay.

4. Roll the brayer over the wax paper, applying pressure to transfer both the ink and the fabric texture.

Note: In this example, some colors were applied by rubbing the bottle tip on the fabric. This translated as scribble lines in the design. You might exploit this to create a look of writing. Also, the thin lines across the tile were the result of a happy accident. Some fabric threads were caught between the clay and fabric. The threads were colored and impressed in the clay.

Variations

1. Moisten a swatch of fabric with rubbing alcohol and drop colors of alcohol ink on it. Brayer the inked fabric on clay.

2. Drop alcohol ink all over clay. Follow with a spritz of rubbing alcohol.

3. Moisten a small piece of felt that is attached to a die or miniature building block with the hook-side of a piece of Velcro tape. Ink the felt with a light color, and stamp the felt on clay in an all over pattern. Fill in any spaces with other ink colors, changing the felt pads between each new color.

Basic Surface Recipes

Acrylic Floor Finish

Acrylic floor finish can be used to create a glossy "paint" or veneer for polymer clay. This technique was contributed by Mona Kissel.

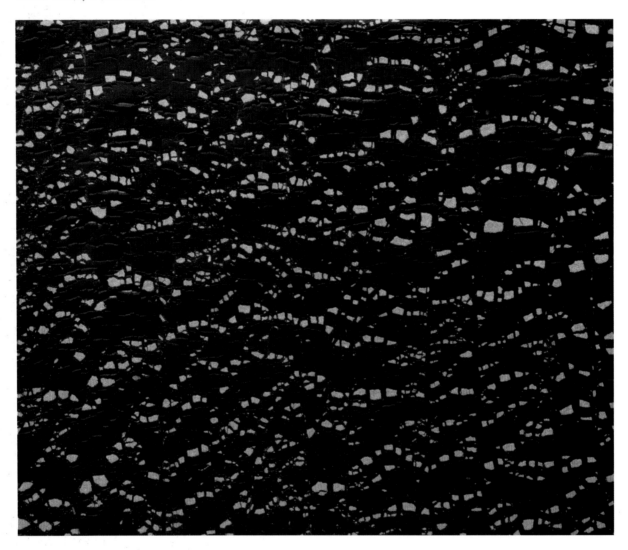

Materials

- acrylic floor finish, such as Future
- metallic powder, such as Pearl Ex
- acrylic paint
- soft craft brush
- pasta machine

1. Mix metallic powder with acrylic floor finish and use a soft craft brush to paint this mixture onto clay.

2. When the surface is dry, roll the decorated clay carefully through a pasta machine to "craze" or crackle the acrylic finish.

Variations

1   Mix both metallic and embossing powders with acrylic floor finish, and apply to clay. When the clay is dry, crackle the finish by rolling through a pasta machine.

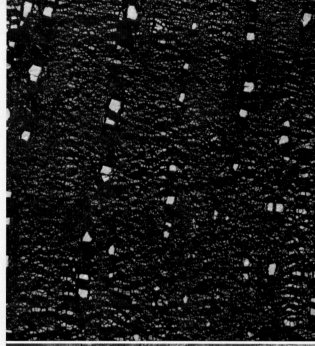

2   Use a soft craft brush to brush on acrylic floor finish over acrylic paint to minimize finger marks or to intensify the color.

3   Brush on acrylic floor finish with a soft craft brush over silk-screened patterns for a glossy shine.

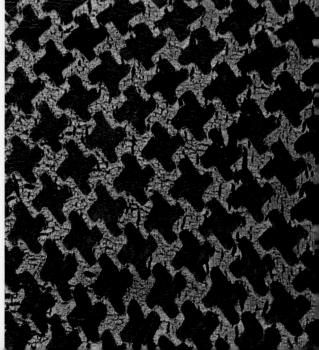

Basic Surface Recipes

Stenciling

Stenciling is the opposite of masking. In masking, color is applied around a barrier; in stenciling, color is applied through selected openings of a barrier. You can purchase craft stencils or make your own using punch cutters or a craft knife. Save the cut-out pieces to use as masks. Silk-screening, which can be found on page 46, is a form of stenciling.

Materials
- assorted tube acrylic paints
- liquid translucent clay
- purchased craft stencil
- squeegee tool
- pan of water

1. Wipe a thin application of liquid translucent clay onto the stencil using a squeegee tool. Lay this treated side on clay, then smooth over the stencil with your fingers to ensure that it is completely in contact with the clay.

2. Using a squeegee tool, apply paint over the stencil. Put the decorated clay aside to let the paint dry. Use the pan to wash paint off of the stencil and squeegee. Dry the stencil and tool.

3. Stencil on three additional paint layers, letting each layer of paint dry before another is added. Applying liquid clay to the stencil helps keep the stencil from pulling up previous layers of paint.

Variations

1   Use stencil plastic and a craft punch to make a custom stencil. Lay the stencil on clay, and apply Crayola Portfolio oil pastels on the stencil around the design. Use a soft, dense sponge to wipe the oil pastel over the stencil and create a design.

2   Use your finger to press embossing powder through the designs of a purchased or custom-made stencil. Keep a wide, soft-bristle brush handy to sweep away excess powder.

3   Apply acrylic gel media to clay with a palette knife and let it dry. Brush on an acrylic ink, then let it dry (shown: Dr. Ph. Martin's Spectralite with Spectralite extender added). The ink brushes on smoothly over the gel, but beads up when applied to clay directly. Note the beading where the end of the violet stripe is applied directly onto clay. Lay the stencil on clay. Apply some gel media over the open design. Apply metallic powder over the gel. Let the clay surface dry, then go over it with liquid translucent clay.

Basic Surface Recipes
Clay as Surface Media

The applications shown are with unbaked clay only, but baked clay can be added to raw clay to create mosaics. Raw or baked pieces can be applied to baked clay to add ornamentation. Adhere raw or baked pieces to baked clay using liquid translucent clay or Poly Bonder and bake again.

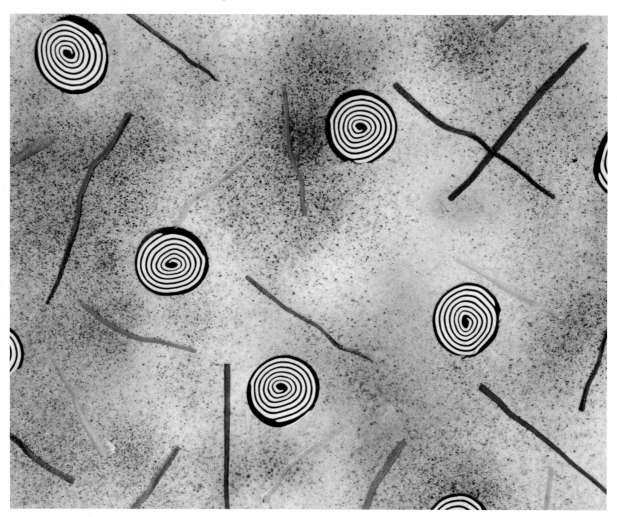

Materials

- white polymer clay (for the base layer)
- small pieces of four colors of polymer clay (shown: violet, magenta, yellow-green, and yellow)
- small black-and-white spiral cane of polymer clay
- assortment of alcohol markers and their airbrush attachment (shown: Letraset Promakers)
- air compressor or can of compressed air for airbrushing
- wax paper
- pasta machine

1. Assemble the airbrush attachment, air source, and a marker.

2. Spray ink from an assortment of markers onto the white clay.

3. Run each of the four colored clay pieces through the pasta machine on a thin setting.

4. Cut and apply thin strips of the colored clays.

5. Cut and apply thin slices of the spiral cane.

6. Cover the decorated layer with wax paper and smooth the applied clay and cane slices with a roller or brayer. Be sure to smooth the layer in various directions to avoid distorting the applied clay and cane slices.

Variations

1   Apply ink from alcohol markers on a very thin layer of translucent clay. Cut out blocks of the inked clay and apply them to a medium-thick base layer of white clay. Roll the resulting sheet through the pasta machine to a desired thinness and level of distortion.

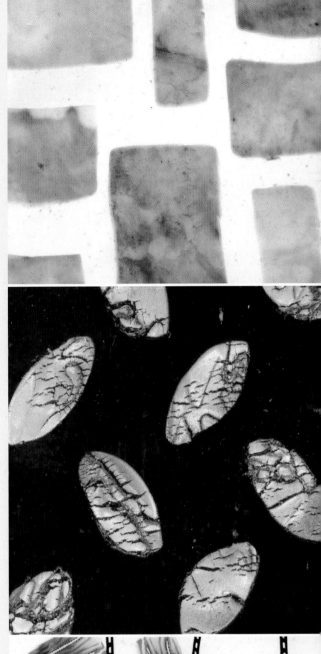

2   Cut thin slices from a mokumé gané block of metallic clay with impressions from cookie cutters and layers of acrylic paint through it. (For more on mokumé gané, see page 24; shown: Stewart Gill's Byzantia metallic paint.) Cut out small shapes from the slices with miniature cookie or hors d'oeuvres cutters and apply them to black clay. Thin out the sheet through the pasta machine.

3   Decorate a sheet of clay with thin canes in a scattered (shown here) or allover pattern.

Basic Surface Recipes

Writing on Clay

When the surface design is not enough, you can write, scribble, or carve on it. Several methods are described here. You may need to practice a bit with either of these methods to get the results you like.

Materials

- rubber stamp with a background design
- acrylic paint (shown: Lumiere)
- acrylic ink (shown: Dr. Ph. Martin's Spectralite)
- assortment of markers (shown: Sharpie oil paint and Marvy DecoColor opaque paint markers)
- artist-grade tissue paper
- detail paintbrush
- ruling pen or Coit single line calligraphy pen
- piece of foam pad or cosmetic sponge

1. Texture a clay sheet using the rubber stamp. (Texturing clay will make writing a little more challenging, so this step is optional.)

2. Lightly sponge on acrylic paint to reveal the stamped design. Let the paint dry.

3. Write on the decorated clay using any of the following methods:

• Add ink to the ruling or calligraphy pen. Write initially on a sheet of scrap clay to test the ink flow. Write on the decorated layer (as shown in the words "dream" and "play" above), being careful not to scratch into the clay. Re-ink as needed.

• Write directly on the clay with the oil-paint marker (as shown in the words "art" and "color" above).

• Lay a piece of tissue paper where you want to write on the clay. Write on the clay through the paper (as shown in the words "create" and "beauty" above).

• Write on the clay with the detail brush charged with ink (as shown in the word "imagine" above).

Variations

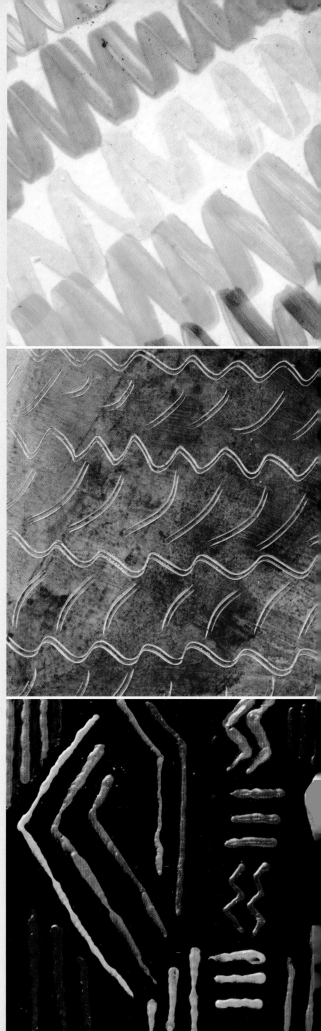

1 The broad tips of dual-point alcohol markers make brushlike strokes on clay. Dip the marker in a drop of rubbing alcohol to wet its tip.

2 Sponge on various colors of dye, paint, or ink (shown: Colorhue dye) and let it dry. Lightly carve into the decorated clay sheet with a needle or carving tool (used here: a Kemper needle tool).

3 Writing with Ranger Crafts' Adirondack acrylic paints doesn't require any additional tools because these paints come in fine-tipped bottles.

Basic Surface Recipes

Spray, Splatter, and Sponge

You can create spray effects on clay through both direct (spray bottle, airbrushing, toothbrush) or indirect (sponge, sprinkled powder) means. The design possibilities are endless.

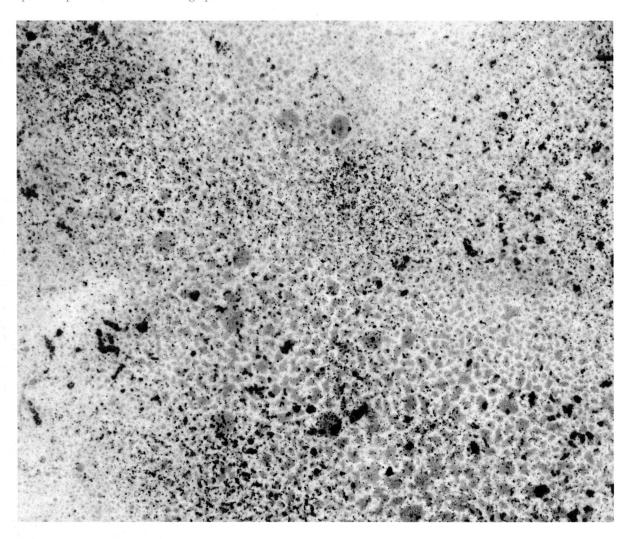

Materials

- fabric dye (shown: Colorhue)
- airbrush medium (shown: Golden)
- chalk pastel sticks
- translucent liquid clay
- small spray bottle
- tissue blade or craft knife
- craft sponge brush

1. Add a few drops of dye to the spray bottle and dilute it with about twice that amount of airbrush medium.

Tip: Colorhue can be diluted with water, but a watery liquid would run off the clay. We diluted the dye with acrylic airbrush medium because it adheres to clay. You can also dilute the dye with denatured alcohol, which will also adhere.

2. Spray across a clay sheet, creating a pattern you like.

3. While the dye is wet, use a tissue blade or craft knife to scrape a fine powder of various colors of pastel sticks over the inked clay sheet. Let it dry.

4. Sponge on the liquid clay before or after baking to seal the pastel. Be sure to apply liquid clay with careful dabbing motions to minimize disruption of the pastel.

Variations

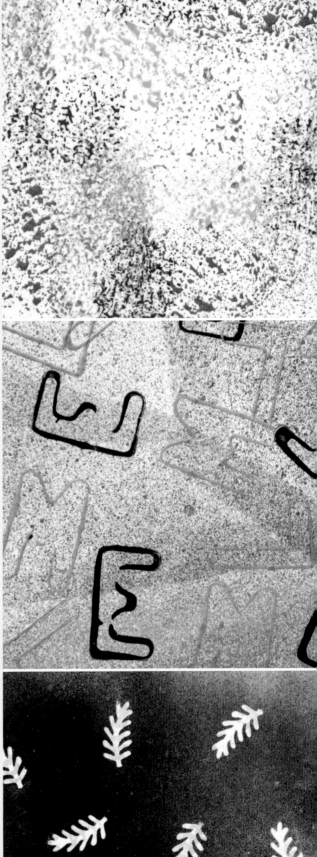

1 With a sponge with a very open mesh, lightly apply various colors of craft acrylic paint. You can achieve a similar look by applying paint with a piece of crumpled aluminum foil.

2 Splatter acrylic ink or dye (shown: Ranger's Posh Impressions metallics) onto clay by scraping a tooth-brush with a palette knife. Mask the clay sheet with palette or wax paper to create a pattern of colors. Let it dry. Use alphabet cookie cutters dipped in acrylic paint to stamp a design of letters on the painted sheet.

3 Airbrush a base color of acrylic airbrush paint on clay, then let it dry (shown: Golden opaque airbrush color). Use a craft punch to make masks out of palette paper, and apply the masks to the painted clay. Airbrush other colors over the clay. Remove the masks. Note: Golden airbrush color will remain slightly tacky on clay, especially if it is applied heavily; however, it dries completely on clay when baked.

Surface Technique Intensives

Once you are familiar with polymer clay, understand how various materials work on it, and are comfortable with some basic surface techniques, you may want to try more elaborate combinations. Here are ten "intensives" to guide and encourage you.

Airbrushing

With airbrushing, fine droplets of paint are applied to clay. In this example, the underlying design in orange paint isn't disturbed by the layer of blue paint airbrushed over it.

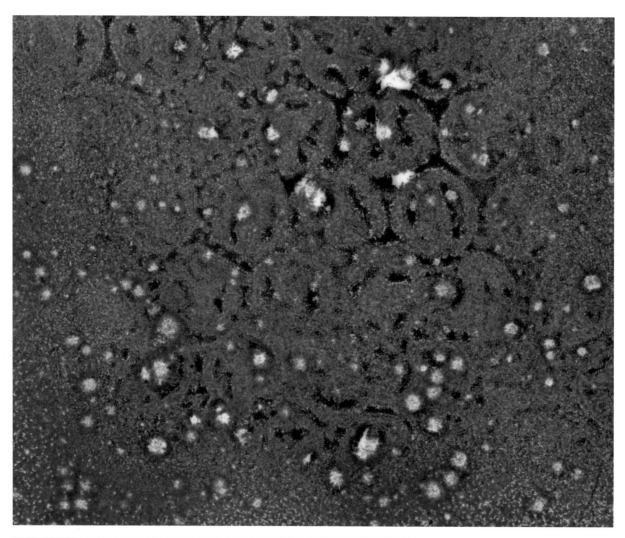

Materials

- yellow, orange, and blue airbrush paint (shown: Golden; you may need to thin other brands with airbrush medium if you are using a compressor with a maximum pressure of 40 PSI or less.)

- airbrushing kit that includes a can of compressed air

- bubble wrap

1. Condition the clay and roll out a medium thin layer.

2. Spray a thin layer of yellow paint evenly over the clay.

3. Spray orange paint randomly over the painted clay. Let the paints dry slightly.

4. Press bubble wrap over the painted clay to create impressions in the orange paint **(a)**.

5. Spray blue all over the decorated clay. The bubble wrap impressions will be revealed as the blue and orange paint mix **(b)**.

> **Notes on airbrushing:** The paint can mist a bit in the air while brushing, so airbrush in a well-venti-lated room. You may also want to use a painting box or hood made out of a cardboard box. One of the best ways to keep your airbrush in good work-ing condition is to run airbrush cleaning fluid through the brush at the end of every painting session.

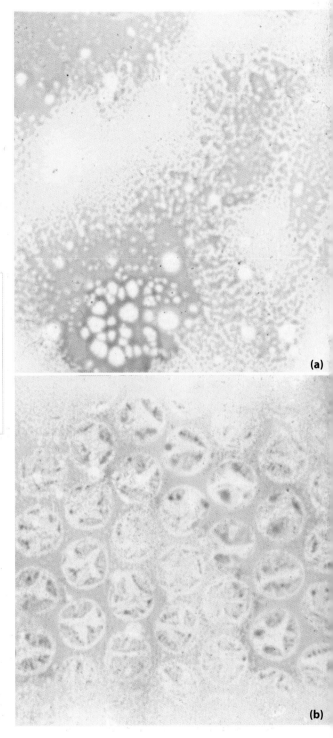

(a)

(b)

Brocade

Paint and a stamped design combine to create either a course or a fine brocade, depending on whether the decorated clay sheet is rolled through the pasta machine or not. Note the variation swatch to compare the results of this approach when using a thin layer of the original blue paint.

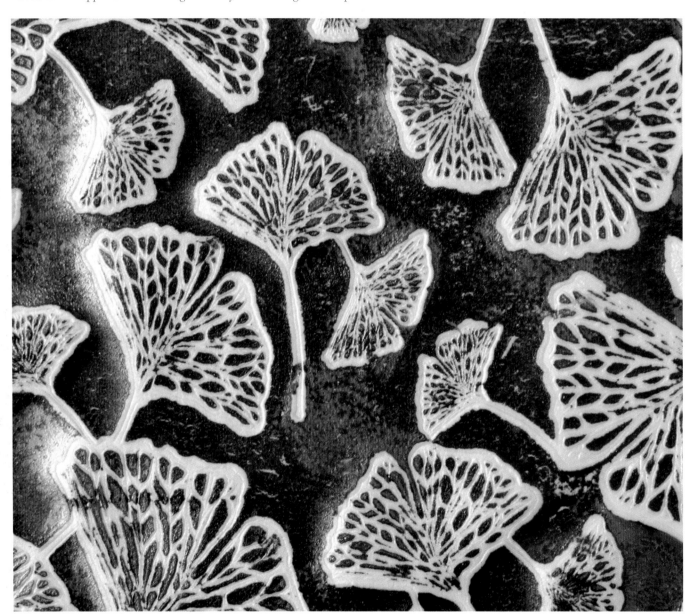

Stamp credit: US ArtQuest

Materials
- pearl metallic polymer clay (shown: Kato)
- metallic acrylic paint (shown: Lumiere)
- texture stamp
- pasta machine

1. To make this tile look somewhat aged, we used pearl, rather than white clay, and change the main paint color. We added a small amount of metallic orange Jacquard Textile Color to blue pearl Lumiere **(a)**.

2. Press the texture stamp into the clay sheet.

3. Sponge or brayer the new color of blue paint over the textured clay sheet **(b)**.

4. Sponge gold paint on sections of the decorated clay sheet. Let all the paint dry **(c)**.

5. Roll the sheet through the pasta machine to thin it. Be sure to rotate the sheet 90 degrees and roll through again to minimize distortion of the texture pattern.

Variation

Here is a sheet done with a lighter application of unaltered blue paint.

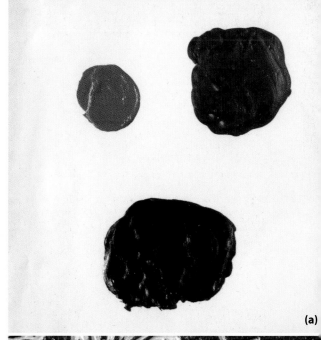

(a)

(b)

Surface Technique Intensives

A Hint of Pearl

Metallic clay alone or in combination with nonmetallic clay offers an array of design options.

Stamp credit: Judikins

Materials

- pearl metallic and black polymer clay
- assortment of opaque and metallic acrylic paints
- background stamp or texture sheet
- cookie cutters
- pasta machine

1. Make a metallic mokumé gané loaf of pearl clay, and place thin slices of it on a layer of black clay **(a)**. (For more on mokumé gané, see page 24.)

2. Stretch the resulting layer by rolling it through a pasta machine **(b)**.

3. Impress the stamp or texture sheet into the stretched clay sheet **(c)**.

4. Lightly sponge on various colors of paint. Be sure to leave areas of the pearl clay showing **(d)**.

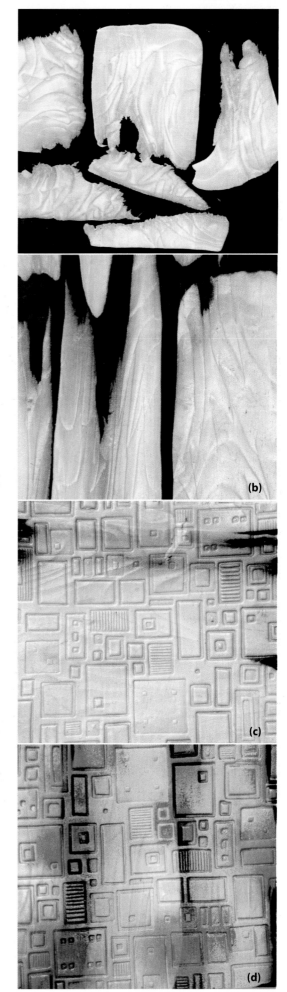

(b)

(c)

(d)

Surface Technique Intensives

Masking with Wire

When masking with wire in clay, or any even paper, you have the option of retaining or removing the impressions made by the mask. Visual interest was created on this tile by varying the gauges of the wire and size of the wire masks.

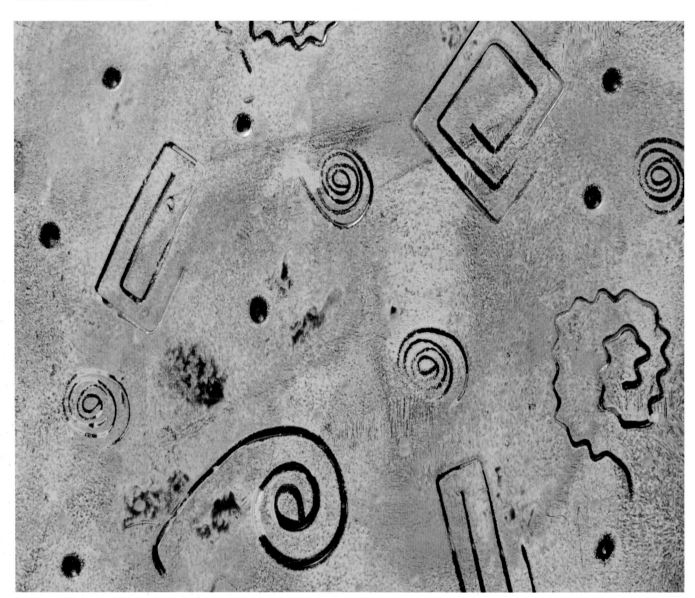

Materials

- black polymer clay
- acrylic craft paint
- opaque fine-tipped marker
- various gauges of craft wire
- square paper clips
- cardstock
- ball stylus
- round- and flat-nose pliers
- wire cutter
- pasta machine
- acrylic brayer

1. Use the pliers to bend and shape the wire pieces as you desire.

2. Lay the wire pieces and paper clips on a sheet of black clay.

3. Cover the sheet with cardstock, and roll over it with brayer to impress the wire and clips into the clay.

4. Remove the cardstock, wire, and clips, and impress the ball stylus over the sheet to add a dot pattern.

5. Sponge or brayer on craft paint **(a)**. Let dry.

6. Dab on a second paint color **(b)**. Let dry

7. Add other colored dots with an opaque marker **(c)**.

8. Stretch the decorated sheet using the pasta machine.

(a)

(b)

(c)

Surface Technique Intensives

Impressions with Paint and Texture

When working with coarsely textured clay, expect that some of the clay will show through the surface application at least minimally. Here the texture pattern and brush strokes complement each other.

Materials

- acrylic craft and metallic paint
- texture sheet (shown: a Shade-Tex texture sheet)
- fan brush

1. Impress the texture sheet into a layer of clay. Paint the resulting clay layer with metallic paint **(a)**.

2. Apply additional metallic and opaque paint colors. We applied blue metallic paint with a fan brush and the gold and periwinkle paints with the straight edge of a sponge **(b** and **c)**.

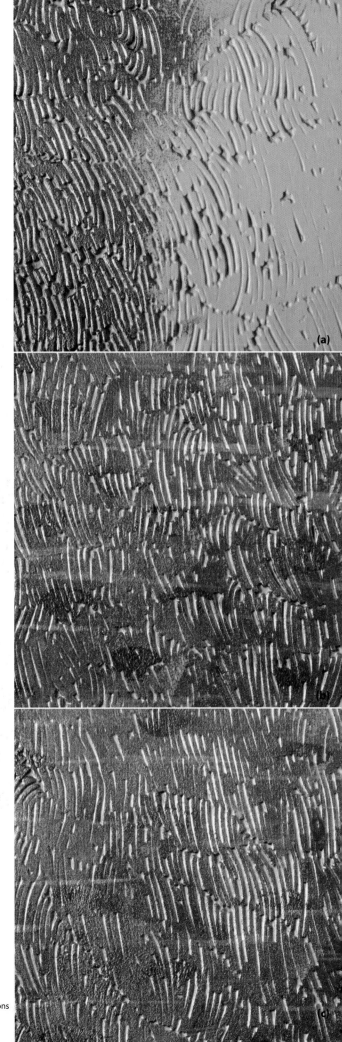

(a)

(b)

(c)

Surface Technique Intensives

Pastel Collage

Sometimes mixtures of clay colors look interesting before they are fully combined. Adding surface design judiciously, so as not to obscure the marbled clay layer, results in a decorated sheet with a bit of mystery and depth.

Stamp credit: Embossing Arts (background); Hero Arts (design stamps)

Materials

- brown, red, magenta, gold, and black polymer clay
- opaque acrylic paint in pastel colors (shown: Sherrill's Sorbets paints by Jacquard)
- background rubber stamp and an assortment of design stamps
- spray bottle with water
- pasta machine

1. Mix small amounts of red, magenta, gold, and black clay with a larger quantity of brown clay.

2. Run the mixture of clay through the pasta machine to achieve a marbled look. See top image **(a)**.

3. Sponge or brayer pastel paint on a background stamp, then press the stamp into the clay. Be sure to press the stamp evenly to achieve good coverage, but try not to impress the stamp in the clay. See image at right **(b)**. Clean the stamp immediately or spritz it with water to prevent paint from drying.

4. When the paint dries, add another stamped image to create a layered design **(c)**.

(a)

Surface Technique Intensives

Gossamer Color

It can be difficult to control the intensity of alcohol inks when applied directly to clay. You can avoid this frustration by applying the ink to translucent clay first and then layering this ink on to opaque clay. When inked translucent clay is left to leach a bit, a nice crackling may result when the translucent and opaque clays are rolled out together. You can combine sections of one inked layer with different compatible colors of opaque clay.

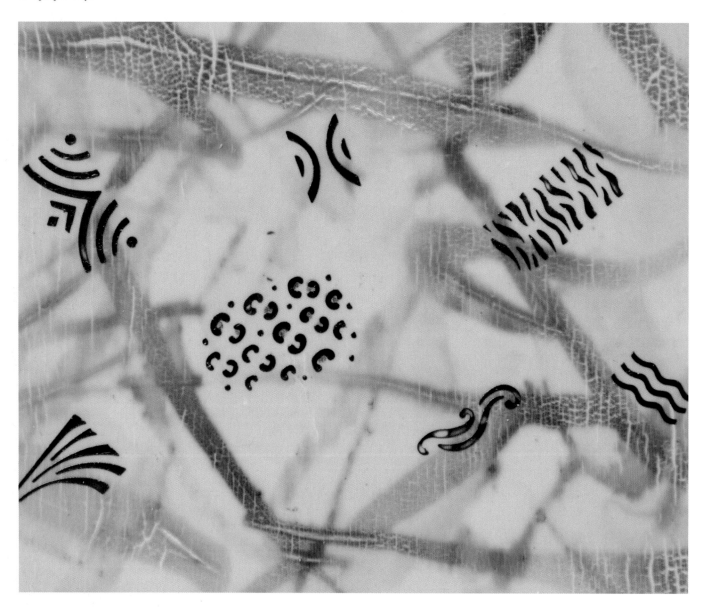

Materials

- beige or ecru and translucent polymer clay (shown: Premo)
- assortment of alcohol-based inks (shown: Ranger Crafts' Adirondack alcohol inks)
- stencils (shown: Createx fingernail stencils, animal prints set)
- tube acrylic paint
- pasta machine

1. Roll out ecru clay on the thickest setting of your pasta machine, then set the clay sheet aside **(a)**.

2. Roll out translucent clay on the thinnest pasta machine setting.

3. Apply alcohol inks to the translucent clay. Let the ink dry **(b)**.

4. Place the inked translucent clay (with the inked side down) on the ecru clay **(c)**.

5. Roll the two clay layers through the pasta machine until the ink is thinned to your liking **(d)**.

6. Stencil designs using tube acrylic paint on the resulting clay sheet.

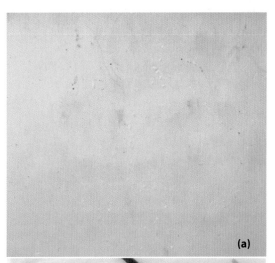

(a)

(b)

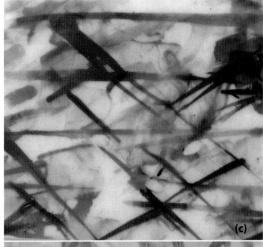

(c)

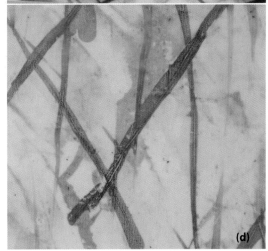

(d)

Ikat Color Blend

Ikat, a form of textile weaving, was mentioned in Polymer Clay Basics (page 15). Here are techniques for creating and using this design. The resulting ikat sheet is embellished with a silk-screened graphic.

Materials

- 8 oz (227 gm) each of white, cadmium red, cadmium yellow, violet, magenta, ultramarine blue, and scrap polymer clay (shown: Premo)
- metallic acrylic paint
- silk-screen stencil (The stencil used here was designed with Photo-EZ.)

1. Set the scrap clay aside.

2. Partially mix magenta and violet clay in a two-to-one ratio.

3. Roll the combined clay and each of the individual colors out on the thickest setting of the pasta machine.

4. Prepare a sheet for blending using the Skinner blend method (see page 23 for more on Skinner blends), with each of the triangles two layers thick.

5. Arrange the colors in this order: yellow, blue, violet, white, magenta-violet, red, yellow **(a)**.

6. Roll the colored layers through the pasta machine according to the Skinner blend method until the colors partially blend **(b)**.

7. Cut the resulting layer across the colors into three equal sections.

8. Stack the sections, staggering the color blend as seen on the cross-section. Cut the resulting loaf in half and restack **(c)**.

9. Roll out scrap clay on a thin but workable setting. Cut slices of the loaf along the cross-section and layer them on the scrap clay **(d)**.

10. Smooth the resulting sheet with a roller, and roll the sheet carefully through the pasta machine, if you choose.

11. Stencil over the smoothed clay sheet.

(a)

(b)

(c)

(d)

Ghost Printing and Batik Effect

With this technique you will be effectively mixing paint colors, so keep color mixing principles in mind. Lascaux Aquarcyl paint is especially suitable for the technique demonstrated here. Other liquid acrylic paints may yield different results.

Materials

- liquid acrylic paint (shown: Lascaux Aquarcryl permanent blue, yellow, magenta, and orange transoxide)
- rubber brayer
- rubber stamps (shown: our own hand-carved stamps)
- needle tool
- spray bottle of water

1. Brayer on blue paint, leaving subtle gradations as shown. Let it dry. Clean the brayer. See image top right **(a)**.

2. Sponge magenta paint along a section of the painted clay. Be careful not to lift too much of the blue paint.

3. While the magenta paint is wet, place a stamp in it. Press lightly to ensure full contact, but do not impress the clay. Lift the stamp. Spritz the stamp with water to keep the paint moist until you are ready to clean the stamp **(b)**.

4. Repeat step three using the yellow and orange paints **(c)**.

5. Write into the clay with the needle tool, tracing around the stamp images.

(a)

(b)

(c)

Surface Technique Intensives

Putting It All Together

Manipulating the surface of polymer clay is one of the many ways to transform the material. With a variety of surface techniques at your disposal, you can transform your clay by applying techniques individually or by combining them as demonstrated here. Whichever you choose, don't be afraid to go further by cutting your finely decorated clay sheet and reforming it or adding pieces of it to pieces from other sheets.

Stamp credit: Earthtone Stamps

Materials

- translucent liquid clay
- assortment of acrylic paints and inks
- chalk pastel
- wire tool
- flea comb
- rubber stamps

1. This decorated sheet was inspired by trying out some initial techniques with a scrap of clay. It became a way to start the tile **(a)**.

2. Texture neutral-colored clay with a flea comb **(b)**.

3. Start applying horizontal lines of acrylic paint and/or ink. Think about adding a combination of dark, medium-light, and light colors. In other words, vary the color (hue) and value (lightness and darkness). Note that there was no attempt to keep distinct lines of color or prevent colors from blending. Also, note that the sheet may not look particularly interesting at this point **(c)**.

(a)

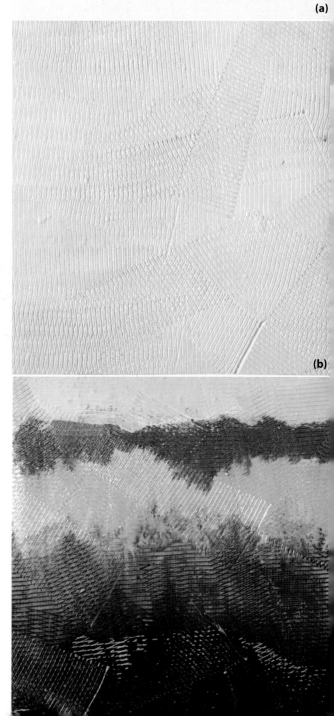

(b)

4. Start adding decoration to each of the paint/ink lines. Add pastel shaved from a pastel stick to moist paint. Add other decoration when the paint/ink lines are dry **(d)**.

5. Completed sheets such as this one could be used as a small wall decoration, on the cover of a book, as part of an altered book page, or as decoration on a box. The sheet (as a whole or cut into sections) could also be used as embellishment for a quilt **(e)**.

(f)

6. You can present a decorated sheet in another way entirely by cutting it and reforming the sections. We cut the sheet into strips, but you might try other variations **(f)**.

In time, as you explore surface design on clay, you may amass a collection of decorated clay sheets. You can create new work with tiles made by reassembling strips from previously decorated sheets.

Tip: Store your decorated sheets between sheets of waxed paper. This helps keep the clay from drying too quickly.

Chapter 3
Projects

This book is primarily about technique and design. While it is great fun to make sumptuously decorated clay sheets, what would you do with them all? The projects in this chapter begin to answer that question.

Offered here are a variety of projects that can be successfully executed by either a dedicated crafter or an occasional one. All of them are very functional and they make terrific gifts (to yourself as well). If you're interested in paper or fiber arts, then you might make the Mosaic Card, Painted and Stamped Photo Journal Cover, or the Arts and Crafts Notepad. If you like to cook or entertain, try the Creative Utensil Handle. You may want to cover other utensils as well. Imagine place settings with decorated flatware! Last, if you like to wear your art, then the Faux Paper Bead Necklace and Tile Bracelet are for you. Both projects are distinctive designs that are almost certain to win you notice.

The projects are useful as learning opportunities because they employ a variety of skills and methods. The utensil handle and necklace projects illustrate how decorated clay can be manipulated to make dimensional objects. The photo journal and card projects highlight decorated clay as ornaments. The jewelry projects are as much about jewelry design and construction as they are about surface treatments on clay.

We hope making these items will fuel your creative energy. For further inspiration, see the gallery section, containing other exemplary uses of surface design on polymer clay.

Project: Mosaic Card

Cut unique shapes from decorated clay sheets and use them to embellish
items such as note cards and book covers.

Artist: Ellen Marshall

Materials

- 2 oz (56.5 gm) of white polymer clay
- assortment of acrylic paints (shown: Anita's in lily pad, olive green, kelly green, rust red, and moccasin brown and Lumiere pearl blue and metallic gold)
- section of embroidery or coarsely woven fabric
- archival craft glue (used here: Crafter's Pic Memory Mount)
- one 8 ½" × 11" (21.5 × 28 cm) sheet of white or cream linen cardstock, dark olive green cardstock with metallic veneer, light brown cardstock with brown marbling, and light olive green vellum
- glue stick
- flat craft or artist's brush
- piece of a foam pad or cosmetic sponge
- rubber-tipped craft tool, such as a Colour Shaper
- ruler
- paper trimmer
- bone folder
- micro cutters (used here: Kemper Ovals set)
- pasta machine

Preparing the Card

1. Cut a strip of the linen cardstock to 8 ½" × 5 ¼" (21.5 × 13 cm).

2. Score the center of the strip with a bone folder, then fold the cardstock in half using the bone folder to make the fold crisp.

3. Using a ruler and a paper trimmer, trim the dark olive green cardstock to measure 3 ¼" × 4 ¼" (8 × 11 cm). Trim the light brown piece of cardstock to measure 3 ½" × 4 ½" (9 × 11.5 cm). Trim the light olive vellum paper to measure 3 ¾" × 4 ⅛" (9.5 × 10.5 cm).

4. Set all paper aside.

Preparing the Polymer Clay Tiles

1. Condition the polymer clay and roll out a thin sheet of clay (number five setting on the pasta machine or $\frac{1}{16}$" [1.5 mm]).

2. Decorate the clay by sponging on some paint colors, smoothing paint on the cloth, then pressing the sections of the cloth onto the clay **(a)**.

(a)

3. Add more layers of paint colors with the brush. Let each layer of paint dry fully **(b)**.

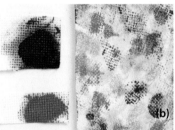

(b)

4. Choose three distinctly different sizes of the cutters and use them to cut an assortment of tiles out of the decorated clay sheet **(c)**.

Constructing the Card

1. Use the rubber craft tool to add a thin layer of glue to the back of the clay tiles as you apply them to the dark olive rectangle. First apply a few of the largest ovals in an allover pattern on the cardstock. Next, fill in the spaces with the medium, and then the smallest ovals.

(c)

2. Bake the decorated cardstock for 20 minutes at 275°F (135°C). When the baking is done, let this cardstock and clay cool.

3. Try out arrangements of the green-gold and light brown cardstock and light olive vellum on the front of the folded card until you like the positioning.

4. When you've chosen a pleasing design, glue the layers, starting with the vellum, to the front of the card.

Project: Creative Utensil Handle

Use decorated sheets of clay, either one piece or several spliced together in a pleasing way, to easily cover utensil handles. Cylindrical handles are the easiest to cover with a rectangular sheet trimmed to fit. A total sheet thickness equal to the thickest setting on the pasta machine works best for most applications.

Artist: Mona Kissel

Materials

- decorated polymer clay sheets
- ice-cream scoop
- wax paper
- pencil or pen
- tissue blade
- large knitting needle
- cardboard baking surface
- pasta machine

Note: Use only solid metal utensils with no plastic components. If there is doubt about whether a tool is solid metal, or whether any plastic plugs were used inside the tool you can test it by baking the tool at 275°F (135°C) for ten to fifteen minutes. The utensil must be carefully watched as the oven gets warm. If plastic was used in the assembly of the tool, the heated plastic will swell and become very visible. This will ruin the utensil, so it is best to work with solid metal utensils.

1. Prepare decorated sheets of clay.

2. Make a template by cutting a piece of wax paper to the length of the handle. Wrap the wax paper around the cylindrical handle, and use a pen or pencil to mark where the paper meets. Extend the line across the paper. This will be the template for the size of the clay sheet needed to wrap the handle **(a)**.

(a)

3. Using a tissue blade, trim the decorated sheet to size using the template. Note: Using this method will result in a clay sheet that seems a bit short at the seam, which is intentional. The tight fit is the most important part of wrapping the handle **(b)**.

4. Lay the decorated, trimmed clay sheet upside-down on wax paper, and bevel all the (inside) edges with the tissue blade. Beveling ensures an almost invisible seam at the joint and allows for smooth edges **(c)**.

(b)

5. Place the clay sheet (decorated side out, beveled side in) on the handle, centering it on the front. This will position the seam at the back of the handle. Place the wax paper between your hand and the clay sheet, and wrap the sheet around the handle, gently shaping the clay sheet to fit.

(c)

6. Remove the wax paper, and use a large knitting needle to roll the clay sheet toward the seam so that the two edges meet. Gently "persuade" the clay sheet to wrap more tightly around the handle. If you are covering an ice-cream scoop handle, as in this example, you can firmly hold the scoop with one hand as you finesse the wrap with the other hand. Smooth the seam by rolling the knitting needle along it.

7. At the ends, use your fingers to taper the ends and press the clay into shape. Gently roll the knitting needle over the edge of the clay to finish shaping the ends and smooth out any finger marks.

8. Finally, examine the clay covering. If the covering is uneven or irregular, very gently roll the entire handle between your flattened hand and a smooth work surface, applying only very light pressure. Pressing too hard will stretch the clay covering and cause air pockets to form during baking. A tight fit is essential.

9. Place the tool on the cardboard with the seam-side down and bake for one hour at 275°F (135°C) in a convection oven. Let the utensil cool thoroughly before handling. To clean the clay-covered utensil, hand wash it with dish soap and towel dry.

Project: Faux Paper-Bead Necklace

These jewel-toned beads with their glass seed beads and metal wire embellishment are opulent and fun to wear. They are reminiscent of the paper beads we made in summer camp, but with a sophisticated twist.

Artist: Ellen Marshall

Materials

- 6 oz (170 gm) of white, pearl, or light neutral-colored polymer clay
- assorted colors of fabric dye (shown: Colorhue silk dyes)
- metallic acrylic paint, such as Lumiere or Stewart Gill's Byzantia
- 22-gauge craft wire (shown: Artistic Wire)
- seed beads, size 8/0
- 2 ½" (1 m) silver-toned chain
- silver-toned clasp and jump rings
- steel mandrels, 1 1/16" (3 cm), or other thin metal rod
- wax paper
- shaving cream
- small container of water
- eyedropper
- foam plate, any size
- paper towels
- block of flower foam, about the size of a building brick
- disposable aluminum baking pan
- cutting mat
- tissue blade
- wire cutter
- needle-nose pliers
- narrow flat-nose or curved flat pliers
- pasta machine

1. Condition the clay and roll it out to be 1/16" (1.5 mm) thin (or use setting five on the pasta machine). Place the sheet on wax paper.

2. Trim the sheet lengthwise. Cut the clay sheet width-wise into long, narrow, equilateral triangles. The longer the base, or shortest side of the triangle, the longer the resulting bead. You can create beads of varying length for this necklace. Set the cut sheet of clay aside **(a)**.

3. Roll the clay triangles, starting at the base of the triangle, on the steel mandrel. Roll all the clay triangles, leaving the resulting beads on the mandrel, and lay them aside on wax paper. The beads stay on the mandrel until after they are baked.

4. Turn the foam plate over so the underside is up and smooth on it a ½" (1 cm) layer of shaving cream. It will be easier to dip the beads this way.

5. Using the eyedropper, deposit a few drops of the dye all around the shaving cream. Start with the lightest color. Repeat with other colors of the dye, rinsing the eyedropper between each color. Drizzle metallic paint over the shaving cream and dye.

6. Roll a clay bead in the shaving cream mixture. Stick the mandrel in the craft foam with the dyed bead sticking up. Repeat with all the beads.

7. Arrange the mandrels in the aluminum pan so the beads do not touch each other. Bake the beads for 45 minutes at 275°F (135°C).

8. Cut lengths of wire that are about two-and-a-half times the length of your beads. String on three seed beads and pull up and twist the wire to secure the beads as a loop at the end **(b)**.

9. Cut the chain to the length you desire, adding in the length of the clasp.

10. Lay out the clay beads and choose the clay bead you want to be in the center of your necklace. String it on to a piece of the wire you prepared. Add a seed bead at the top of the clay bead.

11. Find the center of your chain and attach your first full bead to the center link of your chain. Attach your first bead by using the round-nose pliers to make a wire loop at the top of the bead. Leave a 1/16" to 1/8" (1.5 to 3.5 mm) space at the base of the loop for wrapping wire later. Don't close the loop—leave the wire extended. Thread the extended wire through the chain link until the chain link rests in the wire loop. Wrap the wire closing the loop around the base of the wire at the top of the bead using the flat pliers. Attach all other beads in this manner **(c)**.

12. Construct the necklace by adding the wired beads, one at a time, alternating from one side of the center bead to the other. This way you will see how your necklace is forming.

(a)

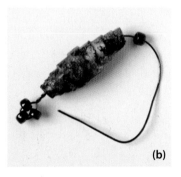

(b)

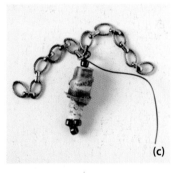

(c)

Note: The shaving cream method was adapted for polymer clay by Gwen Gibson. The author chose to apply the method to the faux paper beads.

Project: Painted and Stamped Photo-Album Cover

This is a great low-cost project in which polymer clay tiles are added to the cover or spine of an inexpensive photo album to achieve a sophisticated design. The amount of fabric required is quite small, so you can splurge on silk and still stay within budget.

Artist: Andi McDowell

Materials

- approximately 8 oz (227 gm) of polymer clay in a color that coordinates with the painted fabric colors (shown: a mix of blue, yellow, and white Kato Polyclay to create a soft green shade)
- various fabric and acrylic paints, dyes, pens, and markers for use on fabric and clay (shown: Jacquard Textile Color, Jacquard Lumiere, and Daler Rowney's Pearlescent Liquid Acrylic)
- three-ring-binder photo album, any size (the album shown is 8" × 10" [20 × 25.5 cm] with a 1" [2.5 cm] spine)
- fabric suitable for painting, such as 100% tight-weave cotton, silk, or rayon (shown: dupioni silk; the fabric should be at least 2" [5 cm] wider on all sides than the combined measurement of the front, back, and spine of the album)
- two sheets of paper for the interior of the album covers, such as cardstock, predecorated scrapbook papers, or your own decorated paper
- 2" (5 cm) tassel with a cord that measures 2" (5 cm) longer than the spine of the album (optional)
- rubber stamps, if desired
- 1" (2.5 cm)-wide foam paintbrush
- tissue blade
- spray adhesive (used here: Super 77)
- hot-glue gun or craft glue
- pasta machine

1. Prewash the fabric. Decorate your fabric by painting, stamping, and embellishing it. In the finished project shown, various shades of diluted blue, green, and yellow fabric paints were painted in 2" (5 cm) freeform waves. Pearlescent paint was added last in arcs of blue. Add any beadwork or embroidery you wish at this stage **(a)**.

2. Heat-set the fabric dye according to the manufacturer's instructions, usually by ironing at the highest tolerated setting, first on the back, then on the front.

3. Lay the fabric, decorated side down, on your work surface. Lay the album faceup and open on the painted fabric. Trim the fabric to create a 1" (2.5 cm) border all around. Miter the corners on an angle, leaving ½" (1 cm) of fabric extending at each corner.

4. If you plan to use a decorative tassel as a bookmark, insert 2" (5 cm) of the tassel cord between the spine and the fabric.

5. Remove the album, and apply two fine coats of spray adhesive to the unfinished side of the painted fabric, following manufacturer instructions. Allow the adhesive to air dry a bit until it is tacky. Carefully reposition the open album on the sticky fabric, smoothing away any air bubbles from the center out. Fold over the long sides to adhere them to the inside of the cover, trimming at the spine where necessary. Tuck in the corners and fold over the short sides

6. Trim your sheets of interior paper so they will cover all of the raw fabric edges on the inside of the front and back covers, generally leaving ¼" (6 mm) around all exterior edges.

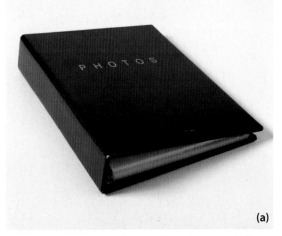

(a)

The undecorated album

7. Condition and mix polymer clay in colors to coordinate with painted fabric. Here we created a medium green by combining white, yellow, and blue clays. Roll out an approximately 5" × 10" (13 × 25.5 cm) sheet of clay using the number three setting on the pasta machine. Fold this in half and smooth out any air bubbles. Roll a second sheet of the same color approximately 5" × 5" (13 × 13 cm) using the number five setting. Paint, stamp, and embellish this sheet of polymer clay to coordinate with the painted fabric **(c)**.

8. Adhere the thin, painted polymer clay sheet to the other folded sheet of clay, smoothing out any air bubbles that may be trapped. Use your craft knife, tissue blade, or shape templates to cut out decorative "tiles" from this decorated sheet of clay. Bake the tiles according to the manufacturer's instructions.

9. The polymer clay tiles can be used as is, or a coordinating border can be applied to the tiles, as shown. A simple striped pattern was cut into strips and applied around the edge of each tile, using liquid polymer clay as an adhesive. Edges were trimmed neatly with a tissue blade before a second baking.

10. Adhere the tiles to the front cover of the album. We used hot glue, but white craft glue also works well **(d)**.

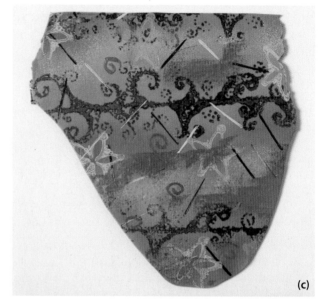

(c)

(d)

Stamp credit: Artist-designed stamps produced by Ready Stamp

Variation

This is another example of this album, using yellows, oranges, and reds. An old credit card was dipped in paint and then dragged over the fabric to create the lines.

Project: Arts and Crafts Notepad

You can make a collection of these notepads for gifts or various purposes of your own. But do keep one handy to jot down project ideas and inspirations, and your list of must-have craft supplies.

Artist: Valerie Wright

Materials

- 3" × 5" (7.5 × 13 cm) spiral notepad
- one block of pearl white polymer clay
- liquid polymer clay (we used Kato brand)
- alcohol-based inks (we used Jacquard's Piñata Colors in sunbright yellow, lime green, rainforest green, and Havana brown)
- Polymer-compatible gloss varnish
- acrylic roller or pasta machine
- pliers
- tissue blade
- small cutter or hollow plastic coffee stirrer
- release agent (corn-starch can be applied with a soft-bristle brush, such as a cosmetic brush, or a mixture of water and Amorall can be applied with a spray bottle to prevent clay from sticking to the texture sheet)
- ½" (1 cm)-wide flat paintbrush
- 5" × 7" (13 × 18 cm) piece of glass
- texture sheet
- nonporous flat surface, such as a glass dish or wax paper

1. Use the pliers to straighten the bent wire end on one side of the spiral notepad. Remove the wire by twisting it out of the holes. Set the wire aside **(a)**.

2. Condition the entire block of white pearl clay. Roll the clay to a thickness of ¹⁄₁₆" (1.5 mm), using the pasta machine or acrylic roller. The clay should be roughly the size of the notepad. Place the sheet of clay onto the piece of glass **(b)**.

3. Apply release agent to the clay sheet. Place the texture sheet on top of the clay and press firmly to impress the pattern onto the clay. (The best texture sheet is one that has a very deep design.) Remove the texture sheet **(c)**.

4. Lay the cardboard backing from the notepad onto the area of the clay with the desired pattern. Use the coffee stirrer to punch out the holes along the top of the cardboard **(d)**. (Trim off the end of the coffee stirrer as it fills with clay.) Use the tissue blade to trim the clay around the cardboard, leaving a 1/16" (1.5 mm)-wide margin around the sides and the bottom of the cardboard. Trim the top of the clay sheet flush with the cardboard. Remove the cardboard from the clay.

5. Place four quarter-size drops of liquid clay onto the nonporous surface, arranged in a circle. Place three drops of sunbright yellow ink onto one circle, then mix the ink into the liquid clay. Place three drops of lime green ink onto the next circle and mix. Place three drops of rainforest green onto the next circle, then mix. Place three drops of Havana brown onto the fourth circle, and mix it into the liquid clay.

6. For this design, begin by painting the outside of the design with the brown liquid clay. Apply a fairly heavy coat so the impressions made by the texture sheet will fill with the liquid but won't overflow.

7. Use the remaining three colors of liquid clay to fill in the rest of the design. The three colors can be placed on the sheet of clay and blended together to mimic the style of glazing found in Arts and Crafts ceramic tiles **(e)**.

8. Keep the sheet of clay on the glass, and place it in the oven to bake. Bake for thirty minutes at the manufacturer's recommended temperature. Remove it, and allow it to cool.

9. Once cooled, apply three thin coats of gloss varnish, allowing the piece to dry between coats.

10. See image below left. Remove the clay from the glass, and place it on top of the notepad pages and backing cardboard. Carefully twist the wire back onto the notepad by twisting it through the holes of the paper and the clay. Bend the end of the wire so it will not twist out of the notepad.

(d)

(e)

Note: The cover is reusable. When all the notepad pages are full, simply untwist the wire, place the clay cover onto a new pad, and twist the wire back on.

Project: Triangle Bracelet

This bracelet could easily become one of your favorites. You may have to remind yourself to glance at it less often. The basic design could be adapted to numerous color palettes.

Artist: Sue Springer

Materials

- one block each of black, copper metallic, red, and yellow polymer clay
- two blocks of translucent polymer clay (we used Fimo Soft)
- black elastic cord
- cardstock
- black-and-white copy of template (page 120)
- cyanoacrylate glue, such as SuperGlue or Krazy Glue
- tissue blade
- wax paper
- brayer or acrylic rod
- needle tool
- ruler
- bamboo skewer
- stenciling brush
- 400, 600, 800, and 1,000 grit wet sand paper
- polishing wheel or soft cloth
- pasta machine

1. Condition black clay by running it through the pasta machine on the number one setting, six to eight times, folding in half each time. Insert the crease first to avoid air pockets. Roll on setting number two, then cut two pieces approximately 2" × 7" (5 × 18 cm) and set aside on wax paper. Condition half of the copper clay, roll on number two, cut into ½" (1 cm) strips, and set aside on wax paper.

2. Combine the following by conditioning until uniform:

¼ block of translucent to ⅛ block of red
¼ block of translucent to ¹⁄₁₆ block of red and ¹⁄₁₆ block of yellow to make orange
¼ block of translucent to ⅛ block of yellow
¼ block of translucent to ½ block of copper metallic

3. Roll red, orange, and yellow mixes to form three 5" (13 cm) snakes, then set them aside. Roll copper mix through the pasta machine on setting number one to form a sheet. Roll translucent clay on setting number one to form a sheet. Cut each sheet to create 4" × 3" (10 × 7.5 cm) sections. Stack the copper and translucent sheets together and roll them through the pasta machine. Insert the 4" (10 cm) side into the pasta machine, first on setting number one, then number three, and then number four. Wrap each snake in a single combination translucent/copper sheet (translucent side touching the snake). Trim to fit, then form the canes **(a)**.

4. Place one sheet of black clay on wax paper, then put thin, diagonal slices of canes in a random design on it. Feel free to layer them or form a pattern. You may cover all or part of this sheet. Use the brayer to roll and secure them as you place them on the sheet. When you are satisfied with your design, roll it through the pasta machine on settings number one and number three. Place this sheet face up on cardstock **(b)**.

(a)

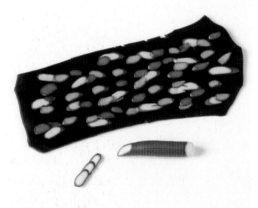

(b)

5. Cut around the paper template (page 120) and place the template on top of the sheet. Mark all the points by poking a needle tool directly into the clay at each point. Remove the pattern and cut the clay with a blade by connecting the dots and mimicking the pattern lines. Remove the scrap clay, and bake the triangles at 265ºF (129 ºC) for 10 minutes, then cool **(c)**.

6. Place the second sheet of black clay on wax paper. On the sheet of black, run the three strips of copper clay in parallel horizontal lines to form channels for the elastic cording. On this arrangement, place the triangle tiles vertically in opposing directions. Press the tiles firmly to the copper strips without distorting them. Carefully trim around each of them **(d)**.

(c)

(d)

7. Peel the three layer tiles from the wax paper and place them facedown on cardstock with the black side up. Place the needle tool in each channel for support, while using the stencil brush to texture the black side of the tiles **(e)**. Bake the tiles for 30 minutes at 265°F (129°C), then cool.

8. Make a snake of black clay approximately ¼" (6 mm) in diameter and 5" (13 cm) long. Measure at ¼" (6 mm) intervals and cut the clay at each mark. Roll the clay pieces into tiny balls by hand and push a bamboo skewer through the center to form 20 small beads **(f)**. Reshape by lightly rolling the beads again. Enlarge holes in two of the beads to later hide knots tied in the elastic. Bake the beads on cardstock for 20 minutes at 265°F (129°C), then cool.

9. Wet sand the front and sides of the tile with consecutive 320, 400, 600, 800, and 1,000 grit sand paper. Buff with a polishing wheel or soft cloth.

10. Put cyanoacrylate glue on the first 1" (2.5 cm) or so of elastic, and let it dry thoroughly. Then trim the end so it isn't frayed. This forms a needle. In two parallel lines, alternately string tiles (inverting every other one) and round beads, making sure the large-holed beads are at the end. Keeping a little tension, knot the string and place a drop of glue on each knot to permanently secure it. When the glue is dry, trim the stray ends close to the knot and tuck it into the bead.

Tips:	Make an extra tile for a matching pendant.
	If the backs of your tiles don't bake securely to the fronts, glue the layers together with cyanoacrylate glue prior to sanding.

(e)

(f)

Chapter 4
Gallery

Ice cream served with this beautifully decorated scoop can only taste sweeter. You can make a scoop like it by following the project directions.

Artist: Mona Kissel

These elegant bracelets illustrate how effectively Mona Kissel uses the acrylic floor wax technique.

Gallery

Tearing effects age the lozenge beads in this necklace.

Artist : Ellen Marshall

These necklaces feature paint and pastel applications.

Artist : Ellen Marshall

Gallery

This necklace is a marriage of metal-wire wrapping and textured clay
highlighted with mica powder. The clay was textured with stamps from
Era Graphics.

Artist: Ellen Marshall

Subtle applications of ink and pastel color soften the hard contour of this necklace.

Artist: Ellen Marshall

Gallery

Vibrant colored clay-on-clay is featured in this pin.

Artist: Ellen Marshall

Acrylic media and metallic paint combine to create the quilted effect on this pin.

Artist: Ellen Marshall

Gallery

These pins are miniature collages of decorated sheets of clay.

Artist: Ellen Marshall

Exquisite seed-bead fringe and polymer clay ornaments (by the author) combine beautifully in this necklace.

Artist: Leslie Pope

Gallery

This artist pioneered the application of silk-screening on polymer clay and introduced methods for building Japanese-style inro.

Artist: Gwen Gibson

Gallery

This artist works with both polymer clay and fiber. She uses surface design in her mixed-media artwork.

Artist: Andi McDowell

Gallery

Stamping and caning applications are featured in this necklace.

Artist: Ellen Marshall

This artist applied her considerable talent as a fiber artist toward designing and making this roll bag. The bag is ornamented with hand-dyed fabric triangles and the author's heart-shaped polymer ornaments.

Artist: Judith Rose

Gallery

The light weight of this bracelet belies its marble-like finish.

Artist: Sue Springer

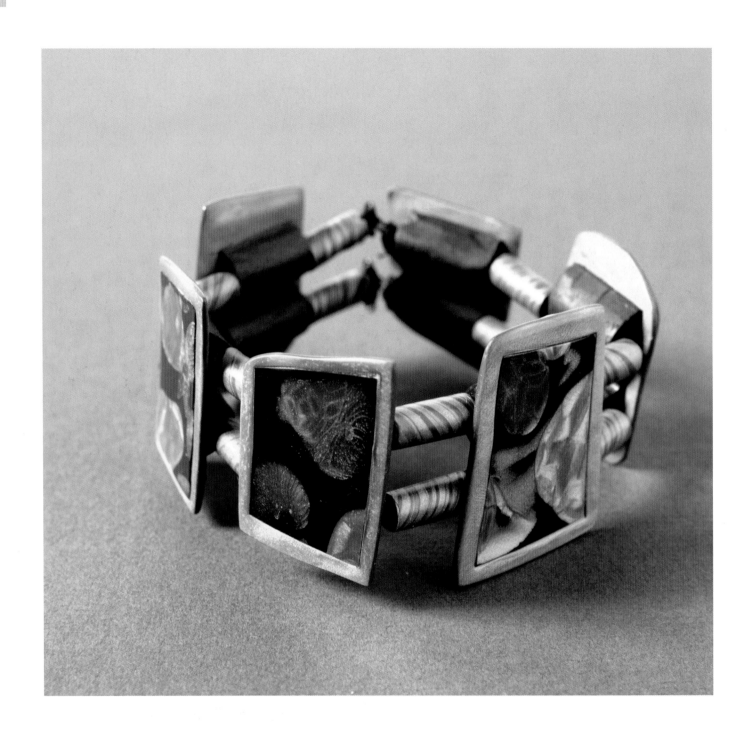

This artist has created ancient-looking, Asian-style boxes with fitted lids. The surface treatment is translucent clay combined with embossing powder and acrylic paint heated with an embossing gun.

Artist: Martha Aleo

Template

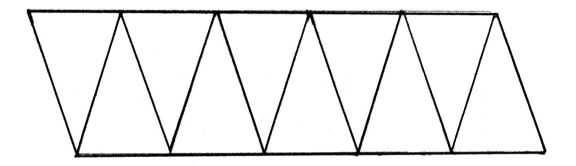

Triangle Bracelet (page 98)

Contributing Artists

Martha Aleo
marthaaleo@yahoo.com

Judith Rose Lapato
jslapato@aol.com

Sue Springer
suespringer@comcast.net

Gwen Gibson
gwen@gwengibson.com

Ellen Marshall
larrine@msn.com

Valerie Wright
valkatdesigns@hotmail.com

Mona Kissel
monak@airphotographics.com

Andi McDowell
andi_mcdowell@yahoo.com

Resources

Polymer Clay, Tools, and Supplies

United States

Accent Import Export, Inc.

1501 Loveridge Road
Box 16
Pittsburg, CA 94565
800.989.2889
email: sean@fimozone.com
www.fimozone.com
general supplies, "Magic Leaf" patterned leaf, molds, stamps, books, crackle finishes, and adhesives

American Art Clay Co. Inc.

4717 West 16th Street
Indianapolis, IN 46222
phone: 800.374.1600
fax: 317.248.9300
email: catalog@amaco.com
www.amaco.com
general supplies, push molds, and tools

Clay Factory, Inc.

P.O. Box 460598
Escondido, CA 92046-0598
877.728.5739
email: clayfactoryinc@clayfactoryinc.com
www.clayfactoryinc.com
general supplies, Cernit, and ripple blades

Polymer Clay Express

13017 Wisteria Drive
Box 275
Germantown, MD 20874
phone: 800.844.0138
fax: 301.482.0610
www.polymerclayexpress.com
general supplies, all brands of clay, and hard-to-find items

Prairie Craft Company

P.O. Box 209
Florissant, CO 80816-0209
phone: 800.779.0615
fax: 719.748.5112
email: vernon@pcisys.net
www.prairiecraft.com
general supplies, Kato clay, and NuBlade Kato and Marxit Kato tools

Aatriceco

12244 N. 84th Place
Scottsdale, AZ 85260
888.484.1999
www.aatriceco.com
Airbrush supplies and accessories

Airbrush City, Inc

24 S. Jarom Lane
Nampa, ID 83687
208.461.9191
www.airbrushcity.com
Airbrush equipment, accessories, technical assistance

Angelwings Enterprises

3065 N. Sunnyside Avenue
Fresno, CA 93727
800.400.3717
www.radiantpearls.com
Primary Elements Coloring System-Polished Pigments and other products

Clearsnap Inc

P.O. Box 98
Anacortes, WA 98221
800.448.4862
www.clearsnap.com
Fluid chalk pigment inks and other products

Create an Impression

www.createanimpression.net
Earthtone rubberstamps, other rubber-stamping and paper arts materials

Diane Maurer

P.O. Box 78
Spring Mills, PA 16875
814.422.8651
www.dianemaurer.com
Wood graining combs, paste paper, and marbling supplies

Dick Blick

P.O. Box 1267
Galesburg, IL 61402
800.828.4548
www.dickblick.com
Lascaux acrylic paints (see www.las caux.com for international sources) and other artist supplies

Resources

D'UVA Fine Artists Materials, Inc.

P.O. 26056
Albuquerque, NM 87125
877.277.8374
www.duva.com
D'UVA ChromaCoal products

Golden Artist Colors, Inc.

188 Bell Road
New Berlin, NY 13411
607.847.6154
www.goldenpaints.com
Acrylic paints and media

Gwen Gibson Designs

216 Bayview Street
San Rafael, CA 94901
415.454.3246
www.gwengibson.com
Photo-EZ stencils, ready-made and stencil-making kits; online tutorials

Heart in Hand Studio

9825 Tarzana Lane
Las Vegas, NV 89129
www.heartinhandstudio.com
Poly Bonder and other tools for
polymer clay

Jerry's Artarama

P.O. Box 58638
Raleigh, NC 27658
800.827.8478
www.jerrysartarama.com
Artist supplies, international shipping

Marvy Uchida

Torrence, CA 90503
www.uchida.com
Assorted markers and pens

PJ's Decorative Stencils

P.O. Box 1555
Newburyport, MA 1950
978.463.5444
www.pjstencils.com
EZ-Cut stencil plastic, and other
stenciling supplies

Ranger Inks

Tinton Falls, NJ 7724
www.rangerinks.com
Adirondack inks and paints, Posh
Impressions inks, and other products

Rupert, Gibbon & Spider, Inc.

P.O. Box 425
Healdsburg, CA 95448
800.442.0455
www.jacquardproducts.com
Dye-Na-Flow, Lumiere, Textile
Traditional, Neopaque, Sherrill's Sorbets

Salis International, Inc.

4093 North 28th Way
Hollywood, FL 33020
800.843.8293
www.docmartins.com
Spectralite and other Dr. Ph. Martin
brand inks

Scratch Art Co., Inc.

P.O. Box 303
Avon, MA 02322
800.377.9003
www.scratchart.com
Shade-Tex Rubbing Plates

Things Japanese

9805 NE 116th Street
PMB 7160
Kirkland, WA 98034
425.821.2287
www.silkthings.com
Colorhue silk dyes, Lumiere and
Neopaque paints, and silk fibers

Tsukineko, Inc.

800.769.6633
www.tsukineko.com
Brilliance ink and other products

US ArtQuest

7800 Ann Arbor Road
Grass Lake, MI 49240
www.usartquest.com
101 light and heavy artist cements,
texture pads, and other products

Australia

The Craftshops Mall

P.O. Box 595
Roseville NSW
Australia 2069
phone: 02.9440.2901
fax: 02.9440.5847
www.craftmall.com.au
General craft supplies, paints and
mediums, tools

Over the Rainbow

ABN: 37 212 817 463
P.O. Box 495
Ascot Vale, Victoria
Australia 3032
phone: 03.9376.0545
fax: 03.9376.4489
email: Heather.Richmond@overtherain
  bow.com.au
www.overtherainbow.com.au
A full range of polymer clay products,
tools, Lumiere paints, and Piñata inks

Canada

Raydec Creations
Warkworth, Ontario, Canada

phone: 705.924.3903
fax: 705.924.3872
Arts, crafts and hobby services
craft supplies and equipment hobby
products and supplies

United Kingdom

American Art Clay Co. Inc.

P.O. Box 467
Longton
Stoke-on-Trent, ST3 7DN UK
phone: 017.8239.9219
fax: 017.8239.4891
email: andrewcarter@amaco.uk.co
www.amaco.uk.co
General supplies, push molds, tools

Homecrafts Direct

P.O. Box 247
Leicester, LE1 9QS UK
011.6 251.0405
email: post@speccrafts.co.uk
www.speccrafts.co.uk
General supplies, Formello, tools, and
cold enamels

The Polymer Clay Pit

British Polymer Clay Guild
Meadow Rise, Low Road
Wortham, Diss
Norfolk, IP22 1SQ UK
phone: 013.7964.6019
fax: 013.964.6016
email: claypit@heaser.demon.co.uk
www.polymerclaypit.co.uk
general supplies and Creall-therm

Rogate Paper Supplies

Bowness Avenue
Sompting, Lancing
West Sussex, BN15 9TP UK
phone: 019.0375.4963
fax: 019.0375.1898
Rubber stamps, parchment craft,
encaustic art, sandy art, quilling, papers,
cards and envelopes

Letraset Limited

Kingsnorth Industrial Estate
Wotton Road
Ashford Kent, TN23 UK
012.3362.4421
www.letraset.com
Promarkers, Tria markers, other products

Stewart Gill, Ltd

Unit 13, Elgin Industrial Estate
40 Dickson Street
Fife, KY12 7SN
Scotland, UK
www.stewartgill.com
Byantia Cloisonne and other paints and
materials. USA sources: www.meinke
toy.com, www.puffinalia.com

Royal Sovereign Ltd

7 St. Georges Industrial Estate
White Hart Lane
London, N22 5QL
info@royal-sovereign.com
Magic color inks

Organizations

United States

National Polymer Clay Guild

PMB 345
1350 Beverly Road, 115
McLean, VA 22101
www.npcg.org

United Kingdom

British Polymer Clay Guild

Meadow Rise, Low Road
Wortham, Diss
Norfolk, IP22 1SQ UK
email: bpcg@heaser.demon.co.uk
www.heaser.demon.co.uk/polyclay/
guild/britpol.htm

About the Author

Ellen Marshall has worked with polymer clay for more than a decade. She is a past cochair of the Philadelphia Area Polymer Clay Guild, which she cofounded, and a past president of the National Polymer Clay Guild. Ellen has been teaching polymer-clay craft for several years and has been published in the magazines *Polymer Café* and *Step-by-Step Beads* and the books *Polymer Clay: Exploring New Techniques and New Materials* and *Polymer Clay Inspirations*.

Acknowledgments

Donna Kato suggested that I write this book. The suggestion didn't resonate with me at first, but as time went on, it felt like a good idea. As it turned out, the process of producing this book both exhausted and replenished my creative well. That was a wonderful surprise. Thank you, Donna. Years before, Celie Fago evaluated some of my work and encouraged me to pursue one of the two directions the work represented. So with simple comments, she has also influenced me and my focus on surface design.

I'm especially honored to include the work of a wonderful group of contributing artists in this book. Many of these artists have not been published before. Some I've known for years and others more recently. But, we are all good friends through clay.

Moreover, writing this book was made easy for me because of the work of Rockport staff. Everyone did their jobs so exceptionally well that they helped create a book that far exceeded my expectations.